Wild
Gardens

Wild
Gardens

Inspired by Nature

Stephanie Mahon

 National Trust

Page 2 Pink *Cleome* and the tiny white daisies of *Erigeron annuus* with cardoons and ornamental grasses at Gravetye Manor in Sussex.

Opposite The border on the top terrace at Great Chalfield Manor, Wiltshire, features dahlias and Japanese anemones in late summer.

First published in the United Kingdom in 2022 by
National Trust Books
43 Great Ormond Street
London
WC1N 3HZ

An imprint of Pavilion Books Group Ltd

Volume © Pavilion Books Company Ltd, 2022
Text © Stephanie Mahon, 2022

ISBN: 9781911657033

A CIP catalogue record for this book is available from the British Library.

10 9 8 7 6 5 4 3 2 1

Reproduction by Rival Colour Ltd, UK
Printed and bound by Toppan Leefung Ltd, China

This book is available at National Trust shops and online at www.nationaltrustbooks.co.uk, or try the publisher (www.pavilionbooks.com) or your local bookshop.

MIX
Paper from
responsible sources
FSC® C104723

CONTENTS

INTRODUCTION

Opposite top An arched gateway in the ancient wall at Great Chalfield Manor, draped in Virginia creeper.

Opposite bottom The Barn Garden at Great Dixter is full of self-sown cow parsley and forget-me-nots in spring.

It might seem odd to put the words 'wild' and 'garden' together. Surely a garden can't be wild? Gardeners spend all that time digging, weeding, pruning and more, in order to tame their plots. However, having strived for garden perfection myself for many years, I am all too aware that despite the effort we put into keeping things in order, to our chagrin, the plants and creatures in our mini domains will still go ahead and do exactly what they wish.

Flowers will self-seed behind your back, popping up everywhere unexpectedly the following season, creating a magical moment you could never have designed. Those dandelions you chide yourself for not removing from the lawn attract bullfinches, who feed on them with gusto as you watch, rapt, through the window. The caterpillars that you cursed all spring, for chomping through precious leaves, flutter back brazenly as butterflies to make you smile all summer.

I think it is these elements of gardening, of life, that are outside of our control, that make for the most thrilling and fulfilling experiences. It is also what makes gardens so valuable in our modern world, with our busy lives and global issues. They are microcosms of the wider wild, offering us a small slice of succour among the fray, and acting as a bridge that connects us to nature. Gardens are

inherently wild, and that is what makes them so wonderful.

In this book, I have chosen to take a broad view of what a wild garden might be, and explore a wide range of places that embody the idea of wildness in very different ways. There are some which evoke natural landscapes, such as Stowe's idyllic pastoral scene; and those that take their lead from their setting, such as The Weir Garden's lush river bank, or the windy shingle-beach backdrop of the garden at Prospect Cottage.

Some are sustainably run gardens that have been schooled by nature – for example, the Beth Chatto Gardens, where her legendary gravel, water and woodland gardens follow the tenet of 'right plant, right place'; and Waltham Place, where everything is managed along organic and biodynamic principles for optimum biodiversity.

Several of the places I visited have an intentional atmosphere of exquisite abandon, such as the gardens in the ruins at Scotney Castle and the gardens at Lowther Castle. Others have been given back to nature completely and allowed to rewild on their own, like Fyne Court.

There are also gardens filled with wonderful wild plants, and those inspired by wild places all over the world, from woodland valleys of rhododendrons at Bodnant Garden to Tom Stuart-Smith's prairie

Left Vibrant azaleas and
rhododendrons line the
path to the bridge at
Trengwainton Garden,
Cornwall.

meadow, and the subtropical and exotic treasures
of Glendurgan and Coleton Fishacre.

Many gardens were chosen because they are
bursting with wild-style, exuberant naturalistic
planting, such as Wildside; or for their irresistibly
romantic air of over-the-top abundance, such as
Beatrix Potter's rambunctious cottage garden at Hill
Top and the dreamy delights of Gravetye Manor.

Of course, I have also focused on gardens that
provide homes and hangouts for birds, bees, bats,
bugs and a bevy of other wild creatures. Gardens
are essential habitats for lots of native wildlife – in
fact, it is said that there is more biodiversity in the
planted areas of gardens than in any other manmade
environment. Colby Woodland Garden and Great
Dixter may seem worlds apart at first glance, but
both can offer important insights into how gardens
are brilliantly beneficial for wild things.

This is developed further in our wild guide, with
lots of advice and tips on how you can make and
manage your own wildlife-friendly garden. Along
the way, we'll also be taking a journey through the
history and philosophy of wild gardening, looking at
everything from plant hunting to the New Perennial
Movement, meadows and forest bathing.

It's time to embrace your wild side.

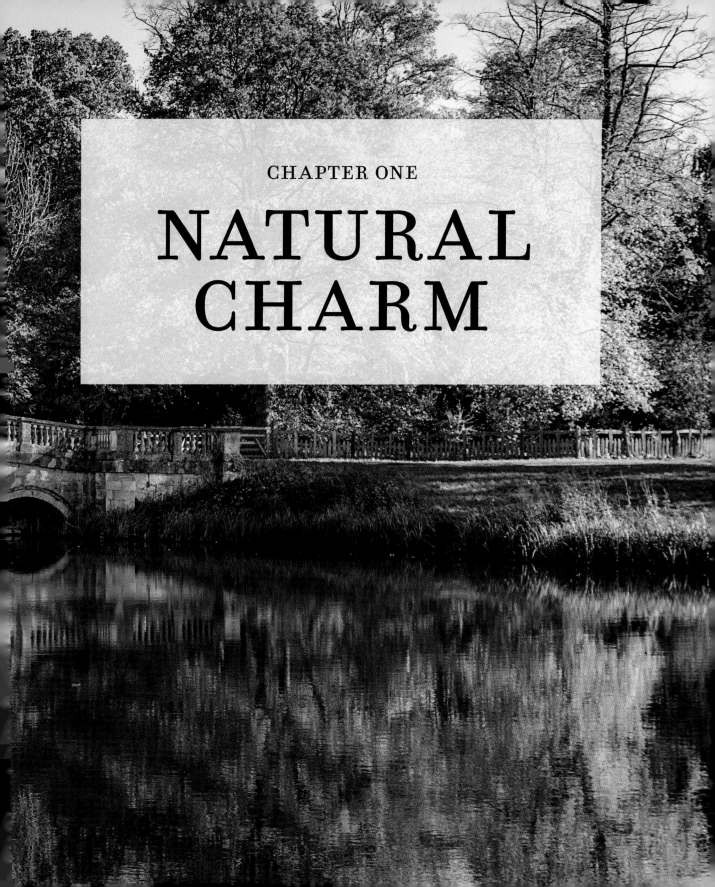

CHAPTER ONE

NATURAL CHARM

These gardens seem almost untouched by the hand of man, at one with the countryside around them, but were all actually carefully composed.

STOWE, BUCKINGHAMSHIRE

Stowe is a vision of pastoral beauty with its rolling green vistas, groves of trees and bodies of water. It seems the very essence of what we consider natural countryside. In fact, it is the birthplace of the English Landscape Garden and a product of human creation and curation – a vast piece of living art in which nature has been arranged to best advantage.

This grand, 250-acre garden was created, for the most part, by Richard Temple, who inherited the estate in 1697. Viscount Cobham, as he later became, spent incredible sums of money over several decades to transform the formal, terraced garden of his father into the most splendid landscape garden in Britain.

Landscape gardens were envisioned as a series of pictures or views, experienced in succession on a walking circuit. Heavily influenced by Classical art and ideals, they were meant to represent the idyll of Arcadia – a tranquil place of simple, rustic, rural pleasures. There were precisely placed temples and pavilions, monuments, statue-topped columns, grottos, ruins, bridges, obelisks and towers dotted throughout, acting as focal points. They often contained coded messages that had to be 'read', such as historical and literary references, allusions to politics and nudge-nudge, wink-wink social satire. Cobham's garden reflected his Whig views, and was

laden with these nods and hidden messages – so much so that a guidebook was published in 1744, just a few years after Stowe first opened to visitors.

Other gardens in Britain and abroad began to copy this pioneering garden, adding features such as a 'hermitage'. There was even a short-lived fashion elsewhere for having a live-in hermit, which soon petered out after one committed suicide and another went on strike.

Trendsetting Stowe was at the forefront of all three phases of the landscape garden, from early efforts to reduce formality and bring the countryside closer to the house, through the Classical style with its temples and codes, to the later Serpentine style with its natural sweeping curves. Cobham spared no expense, employing all the leading designers of the day.

First, royal gardener Charles Bridgeman created the main structure of the garden from about 1714, introducing a lake and a ha-ha – a sunken ditch to separate the pleasure grounds from the parkland and keep livestock out of the garden. Sir John Vanbrugh, architect of Blenheim Palace in Oxfordshire and Castle Howard in North Yorkshire, designed several buildings. The lauded landscape designer William Kent took over in the 1730s with a more informal style, making the Elysian Fields, named for the

Previous page The Palladian Bridge at Stowe was designed to be large enough to drive carriages through.

Below The Gothic Temple above the Octagon Lake. Lord Chatham's Urn sits on an island in the water.

after-life paradise of the Ancient Romans. Architect James Gibbs was brought in to design the Palladian Bridge and several other features.

As if that wasn't enough prestige for one garden, Stowe is also where the famous 'improver' Lancelot 'Capability' Brown got his start as head gardener, in 1741, at the youthful age of 24. Later known for his wholesale, large-scale remodelling of landscapes, including flooding valleys and moving entire villages, Brown began here by working to Kent's designs, directing a team of 40 labourers.

Soon he got his chance to try his own style by making the Grecian Valley, his first landscape design. This valley covers about 60 acres, in a dog-leg shape, with the Temple of Concord and Victory at its head. It appears, like many of Brown's schemes, to be simple, but its gentle contours are the result of complex engineering. His men had to dig out almost 6,500 tonnes of earth by hand and move it with carts and wheelbarrows. He had them plant thousands of elm, beech, Scots pine, cedar, yew, sycamore and larch, and move huge mature trees from other areas of the garden, using a special carriage he designed that levered them out at the roots. There was meant to be a new lake here too, but this feat of creation was beyond even Brown, who settled instead for 'naturalising' the shapes of the existing Octagon and Eleven Acre Lakes.

His prolific output over his career attracted critics, who worried that all of England would soon become a Brownian scene. Why would you spend so much money, they reasoned, just to walk in what was essentially a boring old field with a few trees? It was all too wild, too natural, to be considered a real garden.

These days, Brown's Grecian Valley is a carpet of wild flowers in summer, a meadow that is carefully cultivated to encourage a naturally occurring population of common spotted orchids. Nature may have been manipulated here to suit the whims of men, but she has managed to have the last word.

Opposite The Grade I-listed Oxford Bridge at one with the landscape on a misty autumn morning.

Right A glimpse out across the water from inside the covered Palladian Bridge.

SHERINGHAM PARK, NORFOLK

The Wild Garden is a 50-acre woodland garden within the larger parkland of Sheringham Park, set on the edge of the north Norfolk coast. This estate was the favourite project of Humphry Repton, the man who coined the term 'landscape gardener' and is thought to have created designs for more than 300 gardens in Britain in the late 18th and early 19th centuries.

While 'Capability' Brown had tended to work for the wealthiest and most eminent people in the land, Repton's clientele included the upwardly mobile merchants, manufacturers, bankers and lawyers of the emerging middle classes. Though Repton followed in Brown's footsteps in arranging the land to manage views, his gardens were generally less grand and more pragmatic, making the most of what natural features were already there – no doubt a relief to cash-strapped landowners whose finances were impacted by the Napoleonic Wars. His down-to-earth designs were more accommodating to his clients' wishes and comfort, often with formal areas close to the house.

Repton got the commission for Sheringham when he, supposedly by chance, happened to call in on his son, a lawyer, just as new owner Abbot Upcher was in the office finalising the sale of the estate. And it was only natural, of course, that Repton's other son

should end up being the architect to design and build Upcher's new house there.

'Sheringham possesses more natural beauty and local advantages than any place I have ever seen,' Repton wrote in his 1812 Red Book. He compiled these famous leather-bound tomes for each project, with plans and watercolour paintings showing the 'before' scene, and the 'after' scene on a foldaway flap that could be overlaid on top. His proposal for Sheringham began with the Upper Approach, a long drive along the crest of a ridge through sheltered woodland, which then suddenly and dramatically opens out to sweeping views of the sea, a mile away across rolling meadows and heathland. Upcher considered this bit of flair a masterpiece of landscape design.

It was this woodland drive with its plantings of Scots pine and oak that has developed into The Wild Garden, a habitat for everything from rare moths and slow-worms to woodpeckers and hedgehogs, as well as foxes, hares and deer. It is not called The Wild Garden because of them, however, but to reflect the character of the then wild and exotic plants that were introduced from all around the world. The first rhododendrons were planted here in around 1850, making it among the earliest rhododendron

woods in the country. Now more than 80 species of rhododendron and azalea make up an important collection that offers colour from late autumn to late summer.

The most overt display is in late spring and early summer, when the drive and its side tracks are a candy-coloured assault on the senses, with red, pink, purple, white and yellow rhododendrons and azaleas blooming above a carpet of bluebells. Earlier, camellias and snowdrops put on a show, and in late summer and autumn there are white-flowering eucryphias and the changing foliage of maples and tupelo trees to enjoy.

The extravaganza is further added to with beautiful specimen trees including large pieris, the handkerchief tree (*Davidia involucrata*) and snowdrop trees (*Halesia carolina*), as well as 15 types of magnolia. Some of these treasures were grown from seed collected in the wild in China by plant-hunter Ernest Wilson – Henry Morris Upcher was a keen subscriber to his expeditions at the turn of 20th century.

After wandering in these glades, under arching tunnels of branches and beneath the light-spangled canopy, there is a different perspective to be had from two lookout platforms, from which there are views from above over the whole flowering spectacle, and out across the surrounding countryside.

Above The Temple of Neptune has views across the valley to the house, with the coast beyond.

Opposite Beneath the canopy, a petal-strewn path leads through a tunnel of trunks.

WILDERNESS GARDENS

A wild garden or 'wilderness' was a common feature of many country house gardens in Britain from the 17th to early 19th centuries. Despite the name, early wilderness gardens were actually part of formal pleasure grounds, and not what we would now consider in any way wild looking.

The style first arrived from the Continent in the Jacobean period and was based on the idea of the French 'bosquet', an ornamental grove of trees set in ordered groups, with paths between. The English versions were quiet, secluded areas with natural-looking clumps of trees and shrubs, set away from the house, and often surrounded by high hedges or walls. They were places to walk, reflect and contemplate in solitude, and also somewhere couples could court in private.

The strange choice of name may derive not from the idea of wilderness itself, but from the word 'bewilder', meaning not just to confound and puzzle, but more specifically to perplex with mazes, and cause to be lost, as in a wilderness. These gardens often had mazes to delight and mystify, or mysterious networks of crossing straight and curved paths lined with high hedges, set out in geometric patterns or radiating concentric circles.

One of the best examples of this early style of wilderness can be seen at Ham House in London.

In a re-creation of a 1671 plan, it comprises 16 compartments separated by hornbeam hedges and radiating grass paths, with several summerhouses and a range of woody and herbaceous plants. In the 1680s Charles II created a wilderness at Hampton Court Palace, which was enhanced in 1700 by the famous maze, the oldest hedge maze in the UK.

A rather less subtle creation is the Union Jack garden at Wentworth Castle Gardens in South Yorkshire, created in the eponymous criss-cross pattern in 1713 to celebrate the 1707 union of England and Scotland. There are also surviving wilderness gardens at Prior Park, near Bath, where one could find bridges, a grotto and cascades among the trees; and at Belton House, Lincolnshire, where an earlier arboretum and shrubbery were later added to with an island and boathouse, a hermitage and Gothic ruin.

Over the 18th century, many large estate and manor house gardens developed these sorts of walks, groves and gardens, but by the Georgian era they had evolved to become more informal and natural. At Oxburgh Hall, in Norfolk, the Wilderness created by the 6th Baronet was intended to evoke the idea of an untamed landscape, with trees and shrubs placed to create atmosphere and frame views out across the parkland. Who knows what he would have made of the Wilderness Garden at Knebworth House, Hertfordshire, which is now populated with 72 life-size dinosaur statues.

SCOTNEY CASTLE, KENT

They say art imitates nature, but Scotney Castle in Kent is a good example of a time in garden design where nature was made to imitate art. Possibly the best surviving example of a Picturesque landscape, this garden is set around the ruins of a moated castle in a seemingly fortuitous but, in fact, completely contrived arrangement.

By the early 1800s, people were growing tired of the smooth grassy vistas created by Brown and Repton in the Pastoral style. Gardens should not be uniformly 'improved' in this way, it was felt, but rather take into account the spirit and features of the place and embrace their natural, wild character.

The Picturesque ethos was developed by the artist Reverend William Gilpin and advocated by writers such as Sir Uvedale Price. They preferred things to be a bit more irregular, craggy and shaggy, like the scenes found in landscape paintings by artists such as Claude Lorrain and Salvator Rosa. Gardens inspired by these ideas were supposed to reflect nature, but what they really represented was a carefully composed, idealised version of it – still kindly and quaint, but a little more rough around the edges.

Scotney's rugged, sloping site and old castle were a picture-perfect place to apply these principles, and

when Edward Hussey III moved here in the 1830s, he saw its potential and was determined to follow the trend. He set about building a new house at the top of the hill, and although himself an avid watercolourist, he asked Gilpin's nephew, artist and landscape gardener William Sawrey Gilpin, to help him design scenic views down the garden.

It has changed little in essentials in the intervening two centuries. Outside the New House, which was completed in 1843, the gently sloping grassed terraces give an immediate sense of the wild, left to grow long in summer. Green-winged orchids were discovered here in 1999, after which management practices were changed to conserve them, leading to the garden being declared a Site of Special Scientific Interest.

The most celebrated view can be enjoyed from the Bastion, a semi-circular balustraded lookout, which clings to the precipice above the Quarry Garden. From here, the eye is drawn down the valley, across a mass of rhododendrons, to the tower of the castle, and its backdrop of meadow and woodland rising up beyond.

The Quarry Garden below the house is reached via a multitude of stone steps and steep paths carved out from rearing embankments and sheer faces of rock. When this area was created, fossilised remains of dinosaur footprints were discovered from when there was a sea here in the Mesozoic era. It is rather more lush and green these days, with shade- and moisture-loving plants such as ferns, and colourful shows in spring from rhododendrons,

azaleas and magnolias, and in autumn from hydrangeas and nyssas.

The big central area encompassing the Main Lawns and Lime Walk has been somewhat swamped by *Rhododendron ponticum*. Although it puts on a dazzling display in spring, with mauve-pink blooms blazing en masse all down the slope, it is a monstrous spreader that smothers other plants. There is an ongoing programme to cut it back in stages, open up the view, and hopefully reintroduce choice plants such as kalmias, which the garden was once known for.

By the time you reach the moat, you feel you could almost be in a fairy tale. The water is full of water lilies, and the banks are fringed with

Opposite Inside the shell
of the old castle, a pretty
border of phlox and Japanese
anemones blooms under
rambling roses and clematis.

Right White wisteria adorns
the outside of the romantic
ruins.

rambunctious ferns and rushes. There are large-leaved gunnera and pops of colour from Joe Pye weed, purple loosestrife and marsh marigold, irises and rodgersia. Crossing the stone bridge, the air of gentle neglect is furthered by bunches of red valerian bursting forth from cracks in the walls. This is a good place to pause for a glance back at the New House, high up on the hill above, but it is difficult to look for long at anything other than the unique architecture of the castle in front of you.

Originally a medieval manor house built in the 1370s, it was later added to and rebuilt several times, leaving it as a mishmash of styles from different time periods. Hussey demolished some sections and kept others, to make it into a romantic ruin and the centrepiece of the garden. One section that was

retained was the Ashburnham Tower. Some of the servants were given accommodation there, so they could contribute to their master's fantasy rural scene. The smoke floating up from the chimney completed his living picture.

The ruins are on a human scale, but are infinitely charming with ivy, honeysuckle and roses clambering all over, and a white wisteria draping a whole wall in scented blooms come late spring. Inside the shell, things are more cultivated, if less successful, with a lawn and classic English border that seems out of place. But it can't detract from the captivating sense of abundant dereliction, or the pleasure in seeking out secret corners and peeking through gaps that once held windows and doors.

LOWTHER CASTLE, CUMBRIA

When lauded landscape designer Dan Pearson visited the Lowther estate near Penrith in 2007–2008, he found the shell of a large castle sitting in the remains of a garden that had been reclaimed by nature. The ruins were unstable, and the garden was sad and overgrown. Underneath, however, he could see the bones of a grand old garden – originally laid out in the Georgian era, with some areas later created by Edwardian designer Thomas Mawson.

The Lowther family lost its money in the early 20th century and the estate slowly slid into decline. The garden was used for shelling practice during the Second World War, and in the 1950s the castle, which once boasted a room for every day of the year, was intentionally 'ruinised', with its roofs and floors removed, to avoid crippling taxes.

Current owner Jim Lowther grew up here, and inherited the ruin and a landscape of derelict chicken farms and conifer plantations. He considered selling the lot, but with help from several heritage organisations instead set up a trust and vowed to bring Lowther back to life, asking Dan to create a master plan to reinvigorate the garden.

Dan loved the sense of discovery in exploring these forgotten spaces, and wanted to give other people the opportunity to experience the same excitement, to connect with an old place that was wild, that had been 'consumed by a bigger force,

29

with nature having the upper hand,' he says. 'We have a fascination with places that have got beyond us, where we have lost control.'

This mood, of things being on the wild side, is something that runs through all of Dan's work but, he freely admits, it requires a delicate balancing of the wildness with some evidence of human nurture for a design to feel intended and readable, and for visitors to feel safe. 'If there is a tended environment in evidence, that stops it feeling scary. People need to see a way to be there, even if it is as simple as a mown path.'

His master plan was ambitious, covering 120 acres, with implementation planned over 15 to 20 years. The trust's limited resources were put into reworking a small number of 'hot spots' or garden

areas, while still retaining the magical atmosphere. The entrance square and the parterre in front of the castle with their clipped forms and curated planting are the most contemporary and controlled in design. The further you go into the garden, the wilder it gets.

Jim had visited the Gardens of Ninfa near Rome – a romantic masterpiece set in the ruins of an old village, and the inspiration for countless wild gardens – and was quick to agree with Dan on a similar approach for the castle. They stabilised the walls and planted up, over and between them, creating the extraordinary Garden in the Ruins.

There is a hallowed feel to the main courtyard, with church-like Gothic arch windows giving views out to the garden and estate, and the only roof the heavens above. Plants soften where the walls meet the

Opposite An oak bench
in front of the ruin, fringed
with *Acanthus* 'Rue Ledan',
Centranthus lecoqii,
Alchemilla mollis, *Erigeron
karvinskianus*, jasmine, *Cercis
canadensis* 'Royal White', and
Onopordum acanthium.

Right Native perennial
wildflower meadows have
been developed alongside
the front lawn.

ground and the edges of steps and features, and they
romp up the stonework and columns. You can see the
inner architecture of the building, where the floors
would have been, the old fireplaces hanging storeys
up, and can't help but imagine what life was once
like here. But there is also an attractive incongruity
to having these once indoor spaces now outdoors, a
building become a garden.

This shady but surprisingly windy space called
for a specialist plant palette. Climbers include
clematis and roses as well as a type of Virginia
creeper, *Parthenocissus henryana*, that develops
beautiful silvering on the leaves in low light. Earthy
paths wind around island beds layered up with trees,
shrubs and choice forms of woodland perennials
including *Tellima* and *Brunnera*. It's a predominantly
green scheme for textural interest, with subtle colour
highlights throughout the year. Further in, where the
shade is deepest, ferns and self-seeders, like yellow
Welsh poppies, are encouraged.

Elsewhere in the garden, areas are still being
developed. New lawns have been installed in front
of the castle, surrounded by swathes of native wild
flowers. A new orchard has been created, and a rose
garden was completed in 2019. There are several
previously themed gardens being reworked along the
western fringe, where a beautiful patina of moss has
taken over under a canopy of untouched woodland. In
the Rock Garden, there are plans to reintroduce water
and add shade-loving plants to the existing colonies of
naturalised trilliums and ferns. The Japanese Garden
will be a more naturalistic take on the original theme,
with native Japanese species, and the Sweet Scented
Garden will be filled with fragrant plants.

It's an unusual move to open to visitors while
this is ongoing, but there is something intriguing
about seeing the work being done and the spaces
evolve. Around two-thirds of the garden is actually
being left in its semi-wild state, with only gentle
management. A good example is Jack Croft's Pond,
which was once like a formal canal, but is now being
maintained just for wildlife. In fact, Jim Lowther is
now rewilding the wider 3,000-acre deer park and
seeing an exponential growth in wildlife – a boon
that is sure to increase biodiversity in the garden too.

31

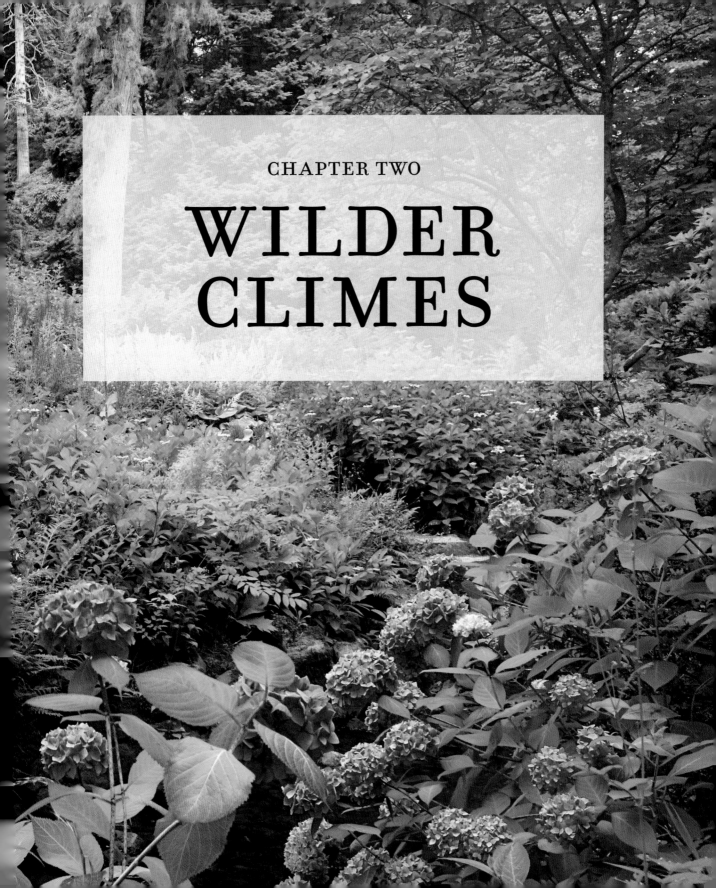

CHAPTER TWO

WILDER CLIMES

Be transported to the wild forests, mountain gorges and tropical jungles of the world, with these woodland, bog and valley gardens filled with exotic wild-collected plants.

TRENGWAINTON, CORNWALL

The international influences on Trengwainton, a 25-acre garden in south-west Cornwall, were there from the very beginning. Sir Rose Price returned to Britain in the early 19th century, loaded with wealth from his sugar plantations in Jamaica. He created the estate in around 1815, no doubt enjoying the mild, moist climate of the peninsula.

The Slavery Abolition Act of 1833, which made the purchase or ownership of slaves illegal in colonies of the British Empire, put an end to the family's prosperity, and Trengwainton was sold at auction in 1835. It passed through different hands until the Bolitho clan bought it in 1867, with successive heirs restoring, improving and developing it. The garden's most formative period was from 1925, when Lieutenant Colonel Edward Bolitho added many interesting and tender trees and shrubs that wouldn't grow elsewhere in Britain but thrived here thanks to Trengwainton's balmy coastal location and long growing season.

Determined to make something special, he asked for help from his cousins, who were enthusiastic gardeners and plantsmen responsible for some notable local gardens. He also received advice and plants from his gentlemen friends Lawrence Johnston of Hidcote and George Johnstone of Trewithen

Gardens. These men were sponsors of plant-hunter Frank Kingdon-Ward's 1927–8 expedition, to Assam in India and the region then known as Burma in Southeast Asia, and they generously shared the spoils with Edward.

Edward's head gardener, Alfred Creek, was a talented horticulturist. Alfred managed to grow the seeds on successfully, with some of these plants, such as *Rhododendron macabeanum* and *R. elliottii*, being the first of their kind to flower in Britain. They were, Edward said, the very founding of the garden.

There are many more rhododendrons here, from tender species to hardy cultivars and hybrids, despite the fact that the fungal disease *Phytophthora* has greatly affected the garden, as elsewhere in the South West. The garden team have had to remove lots of sickly contaminated plants, and have worked with a local college to micro-propagate disease-free replacements, to make sure that this horticultural heritage is not lost.

The experience of the garden is that of a lush rainforest, starting out with the Jubilee Garden's well-designed arrangements. There's a Wollemi pine – a prehistoric tree believed to be extinct until 1994 – mature mahonias and young redwoods, phormiums and hostas, camellias and magnolias.

Previous page Blue hydrangea and pink astilbe on the riverbank of the Dell at Bodnant Garden, Conwy.

Below The Stream Garden bursting with colour from yellow and pink candelabra primulas.

Left Tree ferns thrive in the sheltered, shady groves around the pond.

Opposite This magnificent magnolia steals the show in springtime with its bright and beautiful blossom.

The dimly lit, dell-like environs of the Tree Fern Glade are feathered with the enormous fronds of *Dicksonia antarctica*, and graced with an impressive bamboo corridor. The winding routes of the William Walk and the Long Walk take you around shaded copses and through clearings, over bridges where little streams rush, and past blocks of blue-flowered hydrangeas, fan-leaved palms, trees with textured trunks and intricate, orange-bloomed ginger lilies.

As you make your way, you can almost imagine yourself heroically forging through misty mountain passes, an explorer in full khaki, seeking the next discovery, and inspired by the desire to do your best Attenborough impression. Your reward on making it back out into the open? The view from the Terrace, where on a clear day you can see St Michael's Mount rising from the sea.

The Stream Garden along the drive is a lively, colourful affair in spring and summer, with marginals like giant rhubarb (*Gunnera manicata*), yellow skunk cabbage, hot-pink candelabra primulas and fluffy-flowered astilbe on the banks, along with

arum lilies, ferns, hostas, irises and pineapple lilies (*Eucomis*), as well as euphorbias, rodgersias and Japanese maples (*Acer*), and the striking, metres-tall blue flower spikes of *Echium pininana*.

The Walled Garden has a series of compartments named after the plants growing inside, such as the Foliage and Fuchsia Gardens. This is where the plants get most exotic, and take advantage of the sheltered microclimate, with specimens from a mix of regions and climate zones all rubbing shoulders in a most unlikely and exciting fashion.

One glance takes in *Geranium palmatum* from Madeira and crimson bromeliad (*Fascicularia bicolor*) from Chile, and the next sees an *Athrotaxis selaginoides* tree from Tasmania being consumed by climbing *Fuchsia coccinea* from Brazil. There are begonias, hesperantha, cuphea, impatiens and datura hanging out below *Eucryphia*, *Enkianthus* and *Embothrium*. Further on, one look encompasses magnolias and *Melianthus*, banana leaf and passion flower, and tender shrubby salvias from Mexico. It seems like the whole botanical world is growing within these walls.

THE PLANT HUNTERS

There are plants so familiar, so commonly seen in UK gardens, that people often think they are British natives. But most 'English garden' plants originate far from this green and pleasant land. In fact, the majority were brought here from abroad in a long history of plant introduction that starts from as far back as the Romans, who it is believed gave us box, roses and parsley.

The original English plant hunters, the Tradescants, found plenty of plants to try in the foreign lands they travelled to in the 17th century. And once early glasshouses made it possible to cultivate more tender plants from warmer and tropical climates, there was a craze for growing things like pineapples under cover.

When William III and Mary II arrived from Holland to rule in 1689, they brought a considerable plant collection to Hampton Court Palace. Because of the domination of the Dutch East India Company in world trade, Mary was able to source rare exotics including citrus trees, cacti, palms, succulents, orchids and passion flowers, sending her own plant hunters to the then East Indies, the Canary Islands and the Americas to gather plants and seeds.

It wasn't just a royal obsession. Western missionaries trying to spread Christianity across the world did a little wild plant collecting on the side, and physic and botanic gardens linked up to exchange their prized specimens. Before modern science found ways to extract and synthesise chemicals from plants, these plants were the forefront of medicine, with newly discovered species offering fresh possibilities for beneficial and life-saving treatments.

As well as drugs and tinctures, new plants were able to offer new materials and foods – they were incredibly economically valuable, to the point that they made and broke nations. Wherever countries such as Spain and Portugal conquered, wherever the Dutch and British colonised, from North and South America to Australasia, Southeast Asia, the Himalayas or China, they found things that could further their ambitions, including rubber, coffee, cacao, sugar cane and chillies. The history of plant hunting is tied up inextricably with imperialism.

Exciting foreign species were also of great ornamental worth for decorating the gardens of rich British botany enthusiasts, who sought the thrill of being the first to grow something, thereby showing off their wealth, reach and culture. Lots of new American plants arrived in the 18th century, thanks in large part to one Pennsylvanian farmer called John Bartram, a self-taught botanist who had an

arrangement with a consortium of gardeners and merchants to send back seeds and plants.

Garden plants became even bigger business in the early 19th century. There was huge excitement as nurseries successfully germinated seed and started to grow new plants we take for granted now, such as phlox, asters and fuchsia, and giant redwoods. Nurserymen like James Veitch commissioned plant hunters to go abroad and bring back new plants they could propagate and sell to the burgeoning middle classes.

On their return, years later, from wild, remote locations, these men reported swashbuckling adventures involving dangers such as shipwrecks, pirates, storms, earthquakes, avalanches, raging rivers, disease, civil unrest and being thought of as

a spy or demon by the locals. David Douglas – after whom the Douglas fir is named and who introduced lupins, California poppies, penstemons and conifers including Monterey pine – claimed he wrestled with grizzly bears in the Canadian Arctic. He was later trampled to death by a bull in Hawaii. Reginald Farrer, a prickly character who introduced many alpine species, converted to Buddhism after his time in Asia and was disowned by his family.

Plant hunting reached new heights in the Victorian and Edwardian periods, as more institutions and wealthy patrons began funding their own global expeditions. In the south west of England, in particular, the growing conditions were perfect for creating special gardens dedicated to new plants from Asia, the Americas and Australasia,

Opposite Unusual, exotic plants from around the world were brought to Quarry Bank Mill Garden in Cheshire.

Right A giant redwood tree in the garden at Killerton in Devon, where the Veitch family propagated rare treasures.

such as bamboos and tree ferns. Great horticultural riches were found in the wooded valleys of India, the Himalayan region and China, and so woodland gardening became fashionable.

Availability had increased as the success rates of transporting these treasures improved, aided greatly by the creation of the Wardian case – a glass box where plants could be grown safely, meaning they were more likely to survive the long, difficult journeys back by ship or overland. It was used most famously by Robert Fortune in 1848 on his mission to smuggle tea plants out of China.

The most prolific hunters of this time include Ernest Wilson, who collected about 1,000 species, including the handkerchief tree; George Forrest, best known for several types of rhododendrons, primulas and camellias; and Frank Kingdon-Ward, who introduced the Himalayan poppy, among many others.

We say 'introduced' rather than 'discovered', because these plants were, of course, known about by people before these men came across them – they did not discover them but rather collected them to introduce into cultivation in Europe. They were helped by indigenous porters, interpreters and guides, but there was little recognition of this, or thought given to the impact their plant collecting had on the people, ecosystems and landscapes of the territories they visited. Some were extremely destructive – for example, cutting down a whole grove of rare trees to prevent rival plant hunters from sharing in their bounty.

This sort of plant hunting had a surge after the First World War and then dwindled as upper-class gardening enthusiasts struggled financially. The search for new plants still goes on – more than 4,000 species of plants and fungi new to science were identified in 2019 – but it is more of a collaborative than exploitative venture these days. All living things are now the property of the country in which they grow, thanks to international legislation; and to collect from the wild you need permission, and a licence to sell any plants propagated or bred from this genetic material, with a portion of the profit going to the origin country.

It could be asked why plant hunting is even still necessary. Don't we have enough garden plants to choose from? But the motive for hunting is completely different now. Plants underpin all life on Earth, but two out of every five of the world's plant species are at risk of extinction as a result of the destruction of the natural world.

Modern plant hunters might record where plants are growing without disturbing them, and make plans to protect them, or collect seeds or a specimen to propagate in case the plant goes extinct in the wild. The focus is on conservation, to maintain diversity and support important ecosystems, and in the knowledge that, just as back in the early days of plant hunting, these plants might even hold the key to new medicines, materials and foods.

BODNANT GARDEN, CONWY

Bodnant Garden is positioned auspiciously on the edge of Snowdonia in North Wales, looking across to the grand snow-topped mountains, with glimpses between the trees of the wide River Conwy below. World-class and Grade I-listed, its 80 acres cover formal, woodland and wild gardens, and contain a plant collection of extraordinary diversity.

The park was set out in 1792 as a pleasure ground with walking circuits through trees planted down the hill and on either side of the River Hiraethlyn, which rushes through the lower garden. Victorian scientist, businessman and politician Henry Davis Pochin bought Bodnant in 1874 and worked with Edward Milner on the design of the garden, as well as adding exciting new conifers, including pines and redwoods, from America. After his death, his daughter Laura McLaren and her son Henry McLaren – later Lord Aberconway – developed the garden further over many decades, creating the stunning Italianate terraces that step down from the house and a 'wild garden'.

Henry McLaren was an avid plant lover and collector, and no gentleman hobbyist – he served as President of the Royal Horticultural Society for more than 20 years. He had a passion for all things new, foreign and exotic, and his garden was furnished with many treasures from the Asia plant-hunting expeditions of Ernest Wilson, George Forrest and Frank Kingdon-Ward, including some of the first magnolias to be grown in Britain. When the famous Veitch Nurseries closed down in 1914, it is said he bought all the remaining stock and booked a train to take it to Bodnant. He was also one of the 'Andes Syndicate' of sponsors who paid for Harold Comber's trip to South America in 1925, from which came the Chilean fire bush, *Embothrium coccineum*.

With a climate just like the places from which these plants originated – cool mountain valleys and damp sheltered woodland with high rainfall – Bodnant was the ideal setting for these exciting introductions, but McLaren didn't stop there. He was determined to breed new plants too, and got his talented head gardener Frederick Puddle to create rhododendron hybrids that were hardier, more colourful and flowered earlier or later than the species he had acquired. It is thought that more than 300 hybrids were born and raised here, and although only 115 have been identified in the garden, they make up a registered National Collection.

The East Garden around the house comprises borders, a rose garden, the famous Laburnum Arch, a winter garden and more, but it is the five vast

45

Above The Top Rose Terrace offers incredible views out over the Lily Pond to the Carneddau mountains.

Opposite The Waterfall Bridge is a dramatic, iconic landmark in the garden.

terraces that take your breath away with their steps, trellises and pools, and effervescent planting.

The tall white building at one end is called the Pin Mill, a 1700s summerhouse and later pin mill from Woodchester in Gloucestershire that was transported to Bodnant and reconstructed as a pavilion in the late 1930s. A path behind it takes you into the shade of the woods, and winds down the slope to the Dell. A clear brook, lined with a colourful cornucopia of plants, chases you down the steep hillside, tumbling into little pools and skipping by moss-covered stones. This is the Rockery, a visual sucker-punch of azaleas, acers, hostas and hot pink candelabra primulas, and it demands you take a moment to appreciate it. Yes, it is extra, full volume, nature on steroids, but who cares when it looks this good?

The Dell follows the river's rushing course, its banks layered up with scores of ferns and hydrangeas, camellias and magnolias, rhododendrons – including some red-flowered Bodnant hybrids – and many of the garden's 40 Champion Trees (the best examples of their kind as recognised by the Tree Register). The best viewpoint from which to enjoy the show, whatever time of year, is the dramatic Waterfall Bridge.

Left The Boat House by the Skating Pond at the Far End, originally called the 'wild garden'.

Opposite Herbaceous borders line the terraces that step down from the house to the Pin Mill.

Further along, the Far End with its Skating Pond, originally the 'wild garden', is a soothing place to stroll. Marginal planting, including native plants like loosestrife and reeds, fill the banks, which are visited by birds such as kingfishers, ducks and herons, as well as otters.

On the outer edge of the garden is the Yew Dell, one of its least visited parts, yet one of the most important in terms of plant heritage. This is where many of the garden's oldest and rarest plants, including some of the original ones that Ernest Wilson brought back from China, still reside, in a secluded little glade sheltered by yew trees. Wilson may have advised where special specimens, such as *Rhododendron ririei*, *R. calophytum* and *R. cinnabarinum*, should be placed.

And there is so much more at Bodnant, from The Glades, where spring bulbs including snowdrops, daffodils and bluebells flood the ground beneath blossoming ornamental cherry trees and crab apples; to high-up Furnace Hill with its wildlife-rich woodland; and the three humming and buzzing wildflower meadows, which visitors are invited to walk through barefoot in summer.

It's a garden of history and mystery, with formal flights of fancy and artfully untamed groves, gushing water and giant trees, surprising pops of colour on a canvas of green, and seating exactly where you want it, to take in the matchless views.

COLETON FISHACRE, DEVON

A more perfect setting than Coleton Fishacre is hard to imagine. This 24-acre, Grade II-listed garden lies across a combe, or hollow, above Pudcombe Cove on the south Devon coast, with expansive views of the sea. Rupert and Lady Dorothy D'Oyly Carte, who created the garden here between the wars, chose this remarkable plot from the water while sailing past. Architect Oswald Milne designed a country house to sit at the very top, with several terraces stepping down around it, and landscape designer Edward White helped the couple lay out and plant the wider garden across and down the steep valley.

Unusually for the South West, where gardens are often at their best at springtime, Coleton reaches its peak from mid- to late summer. South facing and protected from winds and salt spray with shelter belts of holm oaks and pines, it benefits from a frost-free microclimate and high humidity – excellent conditions for growing unusual exotic and tender plants.

Rupert was the son of Gilbert and Sullivan's business partner, Richard D'Oyly Carte, who founded the Savoy Theatre and Hotel and built the current Claridge's. He was passionate about the garden, coming down most weekends to check on progress, keeping precise accounts of the works and every plant that was bought – whether from British nurseries or brought back by the couple from their trips abroad to places like Madeira.

The terraces around the Arts and Crafts stone house overflow with an eclectic mix of fabulously foreign plants, from desert-look succulents to the pure tropicana of *Canna* 'Wyoming' and yuccas. Hot borders blaze with bulbine, bugle lilies (*Watsonia*), angel's fishing rods (*Dierama*), bottlebrush (*Callistemon*), pineapple lilies, crocosmia and red-hot pokers (*Kniphofia*), ginger lilies (*Hedychium*), dahlias and alstroemerias, red *Lobelia tupa* and *Salvia confertiflora*. Below the house, the walled Rill Garden has even more tender perennials in pastel shades, arranged in formal borders alongside the eponymous water feature.

The Gazebo Walk is more subtle, with an accomplished medley of texture and form on the banks that slope up and down on either side of the grass path. As well as euphorbias and echiums, fuchsias and *Melianthus*, there are the less familiar delights of kangaroo paw and king protea, *Dasylirion longissimum*, agaves, cordylines and a prize *Echinopsis terscheckii* cactus. The upper storey includes silver-leaved shrubs and the evergreen Chilean myrtle (*Luma apiculata*) with its cinnamon-powder bark and tiny white flowers.

Below The Gazebo Walk borders feature exotic treasures including Chilean myrtle trees and an *Echinopsis terscheckii* cactus.

Opposite The borders around the house blaze in late summer with fiery crocosmia, red-hot pokers, salvias, dahlias and penstemons.

The garden flows out from here with increasing informality, following a flower- and foliage-fringed stream past maples, hydrangeas and a summer-flowering tulip tree (*Liriodendron tulipifera*), down to the lower pond with its large-leaved giant rhubarb, and mature tree of heaven (*Ailanthus altissima*). The sheer face of the quarry opposite was created when stone was extracted to build the house and is now embellished with masses of blue agapanthus.

Above the house, Paddock Wood has been allowed to run wild in an effort to boost biodiversity in the garden. Brambles ramble under the shade of pines; and in the open, long grass is infiltrated by wild flowers and opportunistic garden thugs, pioneer plants and colonisers, including hemp agrimony, deadly nightshade, red campion, elder, crocosmia, nettles and thistles. There are clearings with well-placed benches from which to take in astonishing panoramas of the green shoreline plunging to the sea, with seagulls freewheeling in the air currents above the rocks.

Steps wind down the valley, through woodland groves with tree-sized rhododendrons, azaleas, camellias, magnolias, dogwoods and *Elaeagnus*, to the jungly Tree Fern Glade. The routes back up trace the flow of the brook, twisting and turning around little creeks and ponds, past the Bluebell Woods and the wild birch forest-feel of

Newfoundland, testing your thigh muscles on the climb back up towards the house.

The character of the garden is most easily seen on the West Bank, from where the masterful layering of trees and shrubs in tiers is evident. It should feel jarring to look down upon bananas and bamboos, purple beech and eucalyptus all together, but the arrangement is admirable in its artistry. Yet what are those strange mounds that erupt up out of the wildflower slope below? Mammoth anthills, centuries old. Even here, where the whole valley has been worked to its best advantage, some things are just left to be.

Above Bananas add to the lush tropical feel of the glades at the bottom of the garden.

Opposite: Top left Orange and yellow red-hot pokers (*Kniphofia*) and pink angel's fishing rods (*Dierama*) both originate from South Africa.

Top right A comma butterfly enjoys the nectar-rich pin cushion flowers of *Knautia macedonica*.

Bottom left The devil's tobacco plant, *Lobelia tupa*, originally hails from Chile.

Bottom right *Echium pininana*, the giant viper's bugloss, is native to the Canary Islands.

BLUEBELL WOODS

There is nothing quite like the spectacle of a carpet of blue in the dappled light of a woodland garden in spring. The UK is home to almost half of the world's bluebells. These nodding violet blooms will grow in hedgerows and grassland, but are mostly seen under the canopy of broad-leaved trees like beech, where they find the moist ground and shady conditions they prefer.

This wild, native plant is an intrinsic part of some woodland ecosystems, essential for pollinators looking for an early nectar source. Colonies of bluebells take many years to establish – it can take up to seven years for a flowering plant to develop from a seed. Even then they are surprisingly sensitive. If the leaves get damaged or crushed, they are no longer able to photosynthesise or flower, and may not recover for years. Because of their importance, this fragility and their popularity, bluebells are protected by law: it is illegal to pick them or dig them up, or to propagate and sell wild ones without a licence.

Another issue is the spread of Spanish bluebells, a hardy non-native introduced via gardens about 300 years ago. Native English bluebells (*Hyacinthoides non-scripta*) have narrow leaves, a drooping head and deep-violet-blue, bell-shaped flowers, which are usually arranged along one side of the stem and have a light scent. Spanish bluebells (*Hyacinthoides hispanica*) have broader leaves and stand firmly upright. They have little scent, and the flowers are

more of a conical shape and a paler blue, arranged
all around the stem. The main problem is that they
cross-breed with English bluebells, resulting in a
fertile hybrid (*Hyacinthoides* x *massartiana*), which,
it is believed, is now so common it is outcompeting
the native species, meaning we may lose the unique
genetic qualities of *Hyacinthoides non-scripta*.

The presence of large spreads of bluebells is
one of the signs of ancient woodland – sites that
have been wooded since 1600 and over the centuries
have become thriving, irreplaceable habitats. These
precious places are hugely valuable to both us and
important wildlife, but are continually shrinking
in the UK, with ancient woods covering less than
3 per cent of the landscape.

They are under threat from development,
including building and large infrastructure projects,
and also from the effects of climate change. Wetter
winters and drier summers would mean more floods
and droughts, which would negatively impact many
types of tree. A higher frequency of spring and
summer storms when deciduous trees are in full leaf
means that large trees like majestic old oaks are at
more risk of being blown down.

The changing climate is also likely to advance the
already concerning march of several exotic tree pests
and diseases making their way through the gardens
and woodlands of Britain, from oak processionary
moth caterpillar to Asian and citrus longhorn beetles.

The unfortunate irony is that woodland can
actually provide a real buffer for climate change,
because trees are a natural carbon sink. As well
as planting new trees, those mature trees and
woodlands we already have need to be protected
to keep the CO_2 they have captured locked up.

So, what can we do to help the plight of bluebells
and their ancient woodland homes? An important
part of conserving these vital habitats is having
people support them and protect these sites from
development, but if you do visit a bluebell wood,
keep these things in mind. Stay on the paths and
do not step on and damage the bluebell leaves –
no matter how tempting that 'in the blue' photo
opportunity might seem. Don't take home any plant
material, and clean your footwear and tyres of mud
to help prevent the spread of pests and diseases that
might not be visible to you.

And if you want to grow bluebells in your own
garden, make sure you source English bluebells
– *Hyacinthoides non-scripta* – from a reputable
supplier who has a licence to sell them.

GLENDURGAN, CORNWALL

Welcome to the jungle. Set across three deep, rolling
valleys, above the tiny hamlet of Durgan on the
Helford estuary, Glendurgan is distinctly Cornish,
yet utterly other-worldly too.

The 25-acre garden is enclosed and protected by
its high valley sides, and the shelter belts of trees
were planted by Alfred Fox, the Quaker businessman
who began making a garden here in 1823. It also
benefits from the Gulf Stream, resulting in a warm
and wet climate, and a range of conditions from
damp bog to woodland to dry banks. These different
habitats make for exciting changes of pace and
atmosphere as you move through the garden – one
minute immersed in shade by a cooling stream, and
the next coming out into the open to bask in the sun
in a wildflower meadow.

Narrow switchback paths zigzag along the
verdant hillsides, and views are revealed and
concealed as the garden slopes up and down, over
and across, in every direction at once, like a drawing
by M. C. Escher. This wonderful hurdy-gurdy
topography makes you feel you might somehow
meet yourself coming back.

Glendurgan also has a remarkable plant
collection, with exotic trees and shrubs from all
over the world – the Fox family were heavily involved
in shipping, and could use their network to order

plants and seeds from the furthest reaches of the globe. The garden has since continued to develop its pan-continental approach, drawing on modern plant-hunting expeditions and trips abroad by members of the garden team.

Plants sourced from the wild include rhododendrons, camellias, dogwoods, magnolias and the handkerchief tree from Asia, as well as more subtropical things like begonias, cannas, impatiens and the rice paper plant (*Tetrapanax papyrifer*). There are restios, bugle lilies, pineapple lilies and angel's fishing rods from South Africa, and monkey puzzle trees (*Araucaria*), red-flowered Chilean fire

bushes, cinnamon-barked evergreen *Luma apiculata* and alien-looking *Fascicularia bicolor* from Chile.

Epiphytes, or air plants, including ferns and orchids, thrive on the trunks of trees, mimicking how they grow in tropical rainforests. There are architectural dry-region plants – notably the huge blue limbs of *Agave americana*, spiky *Puya chilensis* and dark rosettes of succulent *Aeonium* 'Zwartkop' – and balmy-looking Chusan palms (*Trachycarpus fortunei*), jelly palms (*Butia capitata*) and Canary Island palms (*Phoenix canariensis*). Rare tender conifer species, gifted by the Royal Botanic Garden Edinburgh, are also thrown in the mix, along with

an olive grove with loquats, kiwis, Asian pears and eucalyptus trees.

Some areas have been renamed and developed to capture the botanical essence of particular geographical regions. In 'Bhutan', there are plants found in the Himalayan region, including a newly identified species of rhododendron, *R. kesangiae*. In 'New Zealand', you will find things endemic to that country, such as *Pseudopanax ferox*, phormiums and tree ferns. A wooden bridge links these areas to The Jungle, where the mood changes to tropical plants with big, bold foliage, such as bananas (*Musa basjoo*), ginger lilies and chonta palms (*Juania australis*).

Emerging out into the open, it's back to Britain with swathes of wild flowers and naturalised blooms lighting up the valley sides. The display starts in spring with wild daffodils, violets and primroses, before bluebells turn the hills caerulean. Columbines (*Aquilegia*) come next, and orchids delight as the grass grows long in summer.

These sunny banks slope down towards the garden's centre, where the squiggly hedges of the cherry laurel maze – almost a mile in length – invite you to wander and get lost just a little while longer in this beguiling global garden.

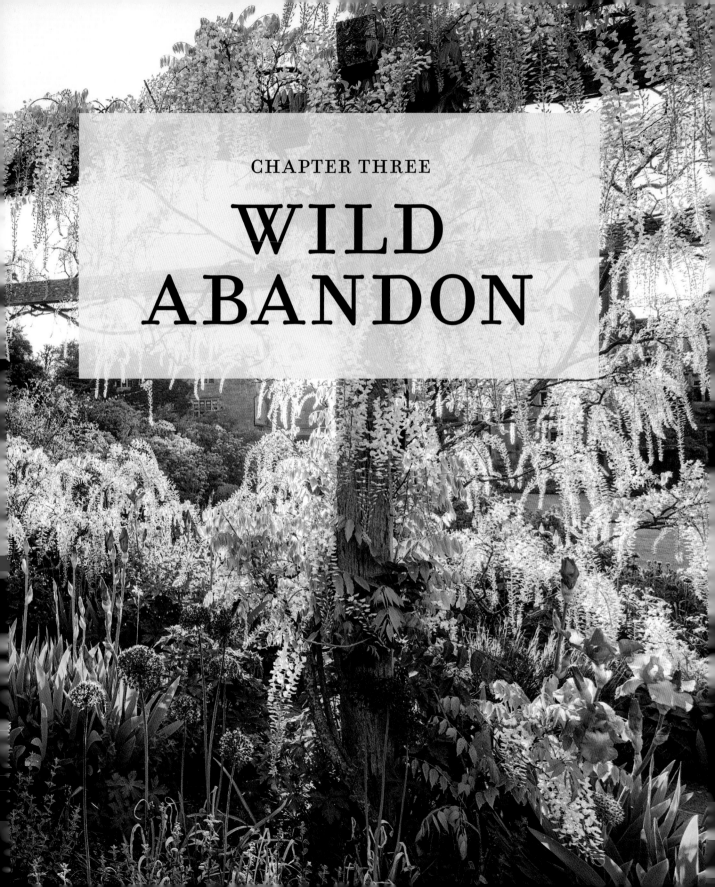

CHAPTER THREE

WILD ABANDON

GRAVETYE MANOR, SUSSEX

William Robinson is sometimes called the father of the English flower garden. He started out in his native Ireland as a lowly gardener, moving to England in 1861 to work in the Royal Botanic Society's garden in Regent's Park, and then, in a stratospheric rise typical of the Victorian era, he went on to become a highly respected horticultural author and journalist.

Britain had been forever changed over the preceding century by the First Industrial Revolution, with the rise of mass production and the rapid expansion of cities and towns. In reaction against this, people began to hold up historic rural life as idyllic, harking back with deep nostalgia to a more wholesome past full of simple country pleasures, more in tune with nature. These ideas were taken up by the developing Arts and Crafts Movement, and still hold sway in the popular imagination today.

The Victorian garden fashions of the time involved high-maintenance, temporary bedding displays of tender annuals in colourful geometric patterns. Robinson decried this trend as wasteful, and published his book *The Wild Garden* in 1870, advocating a more natural approach. His revolutionary idea, which we take for granted today, was to use hardy perennial plants in a practical way

so that, when planted in a place where conditions most suited them, they could grow happily without much care and attention.

His philosophy was not about imitating wilderness or leaving a garden to run wild, but relying on a less rigid design and more dynamic planting style that worked with nature and the existing soil and site, instead of trying to control and dominate everything. In essence, it was about sustainable, low-maintenance gardening.

He was an original thinker, informed by tours abroad to study gardens, plants and landscapes, and was one of the first to promote herbaceous borders, woodland gardens and naturalising of bulbs. In 1871, he founded a weekly journal called *The Garden*, which he edited for almost 30 years, and in which he continued to propound his beliefs, often feuding with rivals in his uniquely opinionated and cantankerous way.

Robinson's crowning success was his book *The English Flower Garden*, published in 1883 (and still in print). Following this, he was able to buy Gravetye, a 16th-century stone manor house set on a south-facing slope, with fantastic views of the surrounding Sussex countryside. Here, finally, was a place where he could experiment and prove his

Left The masterful late spring planting in the Flower Garden includes borders packed with alliums, lupins, sweet rocket, geraniums and foxgloves.

ideas, and he gardened here until his death at the fine age of 96.

Gravetye was left to the State, and the gardens have since been neglected and resurrected a couple of times, and now form the grounds of a luxury hotel. A team of seven gardeners continues to evolve the garden with an eye to Robinson's ethos, while still making it a treat and retreat for guests. Beautifully proportioned, it has a little bit of everything, from formal borders to an oculus-shaped walled kitchen garden.

The central Flower Garden is certainly a surprise, with bright exotics in a raging colour scheme of hot red, purple, magenta and orange being popped in and out of the beds throughout the growing season for optimum impact. This method is known as successional planting, with annuals and tender plants like dahlias and cannas artfully interplanted into a framework of hardy shrubs and perennials. As Robinson was known to constantly contradict himself and defy his own edicts, no one seems to mind the dissonance.

Above this is the actual Wild Garden, where narrow paths skirt heathers, shrubs and grasses, opportunistic spreaders like crocosmias and asters, self-seeders and wild flowers, and even bindweed and ground elder, which compete for supremacy with mat-forming ground covers. A new area on the slope alongside has been developed in the modern naturalistic style, with a fluid display of ornamental grasses and late-summer perennials drawing appreciative glances from diners in the glass-walled hotel restaurant below. Further out from the house, there is more of a sense of the Robinsonian ideal, with meadows, lakes, an orchard and woodland, and views out to the wider estate, linking the garden to the natural landscape.

The Wild Garden influenced many people, not least Robinson's friend Gertrude Jekyll, the celebrated garden designer, who developed many of Robinson's ideas further and in other directions during her own career. His tenets were taken up around the world and continue to be cited today, well suited to our modern need to create low-impact, resource-light, resilient gardens that look good. Over a century on, it's an incredible legacy for a man who started out carrying water buckets as a garden boy – the Irishman who taught the English how to garden.

HILL TOP,
CUMBRIA

'The garden is very overgrown and untidy,' Beatrix
Potter once wrote to a friend about her tiny plot in
the village of Near Sawrey, just a few miles from
Windermere in Cumbria. But really, she loved the
charming ebullience of the garden she made around
the farmhouse at Hill Top, which she purchased in
1905 when she was 39, partly with the royalties of
her illustrated children's books. The author then
spent eight years living between her parents' house
in London and this country retreat, creating, by
necessity, a tumble-jumble garden that thrived on her
part-time attention.

Being from a wealthy family, Beatrix had visited
many stately homes and gardens in her youth, but it
was the more rustic style that she saw in the houses
around the village that inspired her design. Today, it
matches as authentically as possible what was there
in her day – including the plant choice, which is
restricted to species and cultivars that were available
at the turn of the 20th century.

A thin path of variously sized Brathay slate
paving stones runs up the slope from the front gate
to the house, with a large long border to the left and
smaller one on the right. They peak at the end of
June and early in July, with blocks of plants in bright
hues. At the back of the wider border is a simple

wooden trellis smothered in roses and clematis, based on one seen in old photographs. This is fronted by a classic cottage-garden mix of shrubs, perennial and annual flowers, herbs, fruit and vegetables, and plants that some would consider weeds.

First pale mauve phlox jostles with astrantias, geraniums, lungwort, lamb's ears, rose campion, granny's bonnets and ragged robin, before there is more pushing and shoving as soapwort and marjoram rival crocosmia, dahlias, daylilies, globe thistles and Shasta daisies for space. Wild foxgloves and mullein elbow their way in, as do reliably thuggish self-seeders like lady's mantle and opium poppies. Walking up the path, it appears to be a fair fight between all the vibrant clashing colours of orange, white, yellow, purple, blue and lime green, as well as baby, hot and deep pink – gloriously gaudy and gorgeous.

This magical mess attracts plenty of wildlife, from birds to hedgehogs, and for a few years there was even an invasion of rabbits, who overran the orchard and got into the garden by squeezing under the gate. Visitors were delighted to see Peter Rabbit, and the head gardener got to play at being a real-life Mr McGregor.

The wet climate, with up to 1.8 metres of rain a year, encourages other unwelcome guests too, with slugs and snails a real challenge. They chomp away happily at the poor hostas, but the chemical-free cthos here means they are left to it. This open approach leaves the garden purposefully on the verge of wild, with gardening becoming all about managing the balance between order and chaos.

The dark pebble-dashed house is draped in white wisteria, Japanese quince and clematis, and a small ridge of houseleeks – so called because it was once believed that they could prevent buildings from getting struck by lightning. The kitchen garden lies in front, through a green wrought-iron gate that will be familiar to readers of *The Tale of Tom Kitten*.

Left It may not be Jemima Puddle-Duck, but there are glimpses and hints of characters and settings from Beatrix's books around the garden.

Opposite The land rises up from the orchard to the wilder, boulder-strewn hillside.

There are beds for carrots, potatoes, peas, leeks, strawberries and artichokes – not easy to grow in the stony soil. There are wigwams for beans, pears growing on the high brick boundary walls, gooseberries and currants, and the rhubarb patch where Jemima Puddle-Duck tried to hide her eggs. A bee house sits in an alcove of a dry-stone wall, just like it did when Beatrix lived here, and marigolds and evening primrose thread themselves in among the crops.

The orchard, with its big old Bramley apple tree, is a restful pause after the visual stimulation of the preceding spaces. From here, the land rises up into fields of rugged grass with jutting boulders. Beatrix owned the whole hillside, and liked to go up and sit on the rocks, looking down at her house and beautifully shambolic garden.

After the unexpected death of her fiancé and publisher Norman Warne, this was a place where she could grieve in peace. It was a blessed escape from her at times stifling London life with her parents, who had disapproved of her engagement and thought her career as a writer 'improper'. She grew to love her life and the landscape here so much that she became a passionate advocate for conserving the Lake District.

In 1913, she married local solicitor William Heelis and moved to the area permanently. They lived at Castle Cottage across the road, but she always kept Hill Top too – her special space, her personal place.

GREAT CHALFIELD MANOR, WILTSHIRE

The first sight of Great Chalfield elicits that special inner thrill that comes from being somewhere historic, old and beautiful. Tucked away from the outside world in fertile farmland, the mellow honey-coloured manor sits in tranquil splendour behind its own moat.

Originally medieval, it was rebuilt in the 15th century and then restored by engineer Robert Fuller in the early 1900s. The 7-acre garden was created at the same time by the artist Alfred Parsons, who designed a series of spaces around the buildings in line with the ideas of the contemporary Arts and Crafts Movement. However, by the time it passed down the family to Robert Floyd and his wife Patsy, who came to live here in 1985, there were no borders left to speak of.

Patsy set to work on a modern reinvention, with new plantings embedded into the old design. To achieve an evocative, romantic feeling, she kept the existing terraces, paths and walls, but softened this underlying structure with an effortless effervescence of flowers and foliage. Now plants smudge the straight lines and tumble over hard edges. Self-seeding blooms are mostly free to grow where they want. Things commonly seen as weeds, like the valerian growing out of the walls, are left and loved.

It is generous and blissfully unconventional, creating a heady effect.

There are captivating moments throughout, from the 14th-century church in the grounds, where service is still held each Sunday, to the two yew topiary pavilions shaped like giant green jellies on the main lawn. There's a fine old black mulberry tree propped up on crutches at one end, and a magnificent 100-year-old Atlantic cedar at the other beside the handsome Edwardian gazebo.

Steps lead from the top terrace to the herbaceous borders below, from where the garden slopes down in wild style through the orchard to the water. This area comes to life in spring with daffodils and then dark Queen of Night tulips beneath the pretty blossoming apple trees, before the cowslips, camassias and cow parsley arrive. They are followed by long grass and white roses, including 'Rambling Rector', 'Wedding Day' and 'Sander's White Rambler', which scramble up the trunks and through the branches.

The sun-trap Inner or Paved Court, by the old timber-framed section of the house, also features roses, and lots of them, flowering from May the whole way through to October. White 'Bennett's Seedling' and pink 'Madame Caroline Testout' and 'Eglantyne' climb the walls, and yellow *Rosa banksiae* 'Lutea'

Below The landing stage by the water is surrounded by pink 'The Fairy' roses and the orchard meadow.

Left The Edwardian gazebo with the century-old Atlantic cedar tree behind.

Opposite A colourfully planted rill stream that the owners call 'Niagara', with tongue firmly in cheek, is fed by a pipe from the top moat.

grows over the door to the Great Hall, while bushes of scented pink 'Nathalie Nypels' roses surround the central well. Thyme, bellflower and alpine strawberries spread cheerily between the flagstones.

The garden's loose and lovely character belies the amount of work it requires to get this look – deadheading is a constant chore, and each winter is spent laboriously cutting back, lifting and dividing perennials, pruning and mulching with manure. But some areas are lower maintenance than others – on the track behind the stables is Patsy's 'hippery', vibrant in autumn when the rugosa roses proffer their big, shiny red fruit, and dotted in winter and spring with dark purple hellebores.

This path leads round to the reed bed and along the bank of the lower moat, where ducks and herons are frequent visitors, as are kingfishers and woodpeckers. A biodiversity survey here also counted 154 different types of insect.

Spring-flowering bulbs including snowdrops, and summer-flowering shrubs like hydrangeas, line the walkway, which gives the best view back across the water to the manor. The setting for several period dramas, this unspoilt scene, with the landing stage on the opposite bank lined with 'The Fairy' roses, is a final dreamy delight.

Right Delicate pink and white apple blossom transforms orchard trees in April or May.

Opposite The orchard at Barrington Court in Somerset in spring, with apple blossom flowering above white cow parsley.

ORCHARDS

Pretty pink-tinged white blossom, fluttering in the spring sunshine. Apples and pears, damsons and plums, cherries and medlar and quince, hanging plump and ripe on the trees at harvest time. These are just a couple of the incomparable pleasures offered by a British orchard.

We have been farming fruit trees in sunny and sheltered spots since Roman times, but although they exist ostensibly to provide us with fruit, small traditional orchards are actually fantastic places for wildlife, and seen by conservation experts as 'priority' habitats.

Unlike commercial orchards, which are densely planted to produce large crops, the trees in traditional orchards are spaced further apart. The grass underneath is often managed like a meadow, and the plot bounded with informal shaggy hedgerows of mixed native shrubs.

This marvellous mix, and its low-maintenance management, attracts an abundance of creatures.

Bees of all types pollinate the delicate spring blossom in exchange for a feast of early nectar and pollen, and butterflies and other pollinators gorge themselves on the wild flowers below. Birds such as blackbirds and thrushes eat the fruit on the trees, and badgers, foxes, hedgehogs, brown rats, voles, mice and other mammals forage for it when it falls. Lesser spotted woodpeckers nest and bats roost in the trees, and older specimens with veteran features like hollow trunks and split bark are loved by fungi and insects such as the rare noble chafer beetle. The trees are also host to lichen, and mistletoe, which supports the mistletoe marble moth.

As well as a source of food and drinks for us, these orchards are home to heritage and rare local fruit varieties with fabulously evocative names like

'Slack-ma-Girdle' and 'Jackets and Petticoats' that need to be conserved. Sadly, the number of traditional orchards is in sharp decline – about 60 per cent in England have disappeared since 1950. This is partly down to increasing development, and to changes in farming. We rarely hear delicious words such as 'wassailing' and 'scrumping' anymore.

The National Trust looks after nearly 200 orchards, and has pledged to create 68 new ones by 2025. Community-focused organisations, such as The Orchard Project and the People's Trust for Endangered Species, are committed to preserving and promoting orchards' special place in our landscape. You can help by supporting fruit, juice and cider sales from your local orchard, or maybe volunteer your time to care for these multi-layered mosaic habitats that sustain so much life.

SISSINGHURST CASTLE, KENT

No selection of wildly romantic gardens could omit the grand dame, Sissinghurst. World famous – a garden icon – it is the epitome of the exuberantly planted English style, built on the ideas of earlier Arts and Crafts gardens, but with a true sense of place.

The poet and writer Vita Sackville-West and her husband Harold Nicolson, diplomat and politician, came to view the place in spring 1930, when it was uninhabitable, little more than a ruin. When they saw the tower of two turrets, still standing from Elizabethan times, the moat and the overgrown grounds set in wide Weald farmland, it was love at first sight.

The garden layout was planned by Harold as a series of rooms with axial paths, which Vita then filled to the brim with planting based on different, usually colour, themes. This was a perfect marriage of formal design, with framing walls and hedges, around lavish, full beds and borders, every inch packed with blooms … and then a bit more crammed in for good measure. It is this contrast, of the strict linear restraint of the design and the vivacious planting, that has such a potent effect.

There's also a nod to that imagined rural past, creating a wistful atmosphere that has captivated visitors down the decades. You feel it from the moment you walk through the entrance archway to the courtyard and are drawn to look up at the tower, where Vita had her writing room. It is most evident in the Rose Garden, where a voluptuous display in rich shades is dominated by climbing, rambling, shrub and bush roses, planted 'recklessly' in the spirit of Vita, interspersed with perennials including foxgloves, lupins, peonies, alliums and irises.

The Lime Walk was Harold's favourite room, and speaks of his orderliness, with pleached lime trees set along the stone path. Around their toes and down the sides of the space grow masses of spring-flowering bulbs, with yellow daffodils and blue muscari, and bright tulips in large terracotta pots set at intervals down its length.

The bold and vibrant Cottage Garden features flowers in sunset shades of yellow, orange and red, while the much-imitated White Garden sticks to pale blooms and a range of foliage in green, silver and grey. There's the Moat Walk, where an ancient brick wall froths with white wisteria, and mauve wallflowers surge from the cracks; a scented Herb Garden; and the Delos area, with a Mediterranean feel, inspired by Greek olive groves.

Below Irises grow along the moat which runs from the garden out along the Orchard.

Right The Nuttery in late spring, with shuttlecock ferns, fritillaries and a bevy of beautiful blue- and white-flowered bulbs and woodland plants.

Opposite Romantic borders of roses and foxgloves in the Rose Garden in summer.

But it is perhaps the Nuttery – the spot that persuaded Harold and Vita to buy Sissinghurst that day in 1930 – that most evokes a sort of nostalgia for lost nature. Underplanted for many years with primroses, this old 'plat' or nut orchard of Kentish cobnuts is now a stylised woodland garden alive with a succession of shade-loving spring plants, from early anemones to oxslips and violets, through shuttlecock ferns and blue *Omphalodes*. They are joined by lime-yellow *Smyrnium* and *Euphorbia*, white Spanish bluebells and trilliums, and exciting rare *Veratrum*.

The Orchard is where things get much more informal, where the wildness is given its head. Drifts of daffodils decorate the grass in spring, along with snake's head fritillaries, before the apple trees blossom above in opulent profusion. Vita took inspiration from William Robinson and planted rambling roses around the old trees, and now they cling to the trunks and trail foaming boughs of white and pink in summer. The grass grows long beneath and is being restored to native wildflower meadow, with neat paths cut through for strolling, and a bench from which to take in the bucolic scene. An in-between space, suspended in time, the Orchard helps the garden transition out into the surrounding countryside, and fulfils our latent yearning for a mythical English Eden.

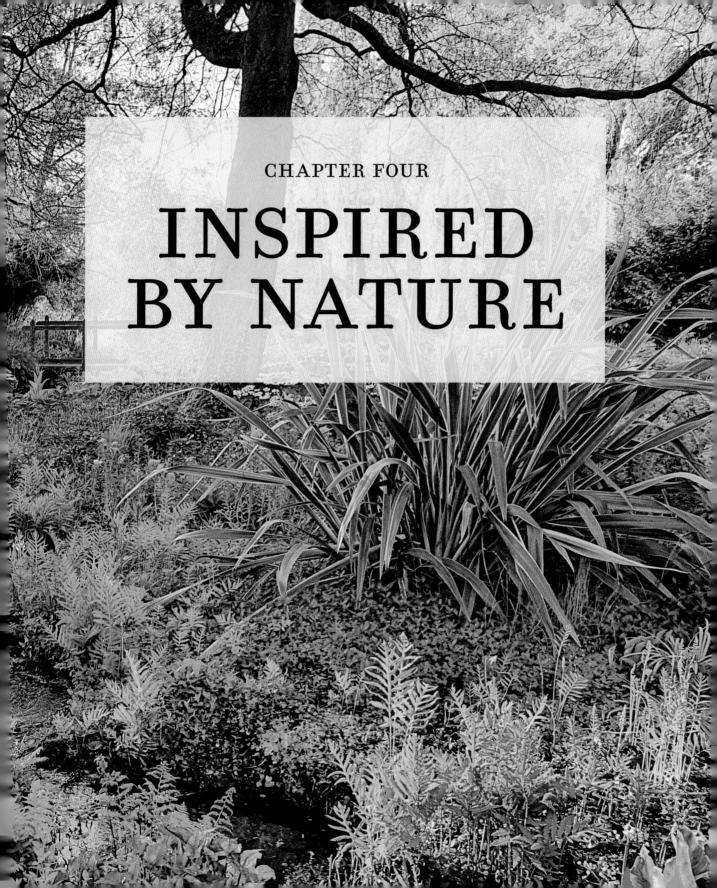

CHAPTER FOUR

INSPIRED BY NATURE

These garden makers work with nature and grow plants in a naturalistic style, inspired by wild plant communities.

BETH CHATTO GARDENS, ESSEX

Beth Chatto may not have been the first to advise 'right plant, right place', but it is certainly the ethos for which she is best known. The late gardener and nurserywoman was promoting ecological planting and sustainable gardening practices long before those were recognisable terms, trusting her own instincts to create a groundbreaking garden in the dry, flat farmland of Essex.

Her husband Andrew was a fruit farmer with a deep interest in plants from all over the world, and Beth loved floristry and gardening. His passion for botanical research and her artistic approach made for a winning team. In 1960, they moved to this patch of unused ground – which Beth described as an 'overgrown wasteland' – surrounded by apple orchards, with poor, sandy soil at one end and a spring-fed ditch at the other. They built a house and began making a garden around it – a challenge in this area of East Anglia, which receives only 50cm of rain a year, and where hosepipe bans are not uncommon.

Beth decided to accept her climate and situation, and let the growing conditions dictate what plants to grow. She created a shaded woodland garden under trees, a water garden in the damp area, and a dry garden where it was free draining. To her, it was just common sense to grow what suited the soil, instead of trying to change it, or constantly feed and water.

This may seem obvious now, but when Beth started her nursery in 1967, high horticulture was about highly bred plants and uber-cultivated gardens. The initial reaction to her plant stand at flower shows like Chelsea demonstrates how unusual her ideas were to the gardening establishment – there's a story that she was almost disqualified from exhibiting when one judge dismissed her wild-feel plants as nothing but weeds. She then won 10 successive Chelsea Gold medals in the 1970s.

She also felt that garden plants should do more than just one thing. Flower colour – sure, it's important, but foliage throughout the season is too, as are contrasting textures, shapes and forms. This is most apparent in her experimental Gravel Garden, which she made on the site of an old car park in 1991. The inspiration came from a dried-up river bed she saw on a trip to New Zealand with Christopher Lloyd of Great Dixter, East Sussex, and a visit they made to Dungeness in Kent, where by chance they met and were impressed by Derek Jarman and his garden at Prospect Cottage.

The plants don't grow directly in the gravel in Beth Chatto's garden, but send their roots down through it to the soil below. To prepare the area, the compacted earth was dug over and compost was added to give the plants a chance to establish, before the half-acre area was covered with a 4cm-deep mulch of sand and gravel.

Beth's plant list wasn't restricted to things from just one part of the world, and she wasn't trying to emulate an actual natural landscape. The focus was on finding drought-tolerant plants she could use to create a beautifully designed garden that looked good all year, but wouldn't need additional care and resources. Her choices were often structural and evergreen, with small foliage or grey-green, glaucous or succulent leaves, and came mostly from Mediterranean-climate zones such as Central Chile, the Mediterranean Basin and the Cape Region of South Africa. There is a backbone of shrubs and trees which offers height, and then an understorey of softly mounded sub-shrubs, flowering perennials and bulbs which peaks from late May and early June into summer. Interest continues into autumn with fiery foliage and ornamental grasses.

The Water Garden was a boggy hollow before Beth had four ponds dug, imitating a cloud formation she had seen. It's a peaceful spot after the invigoration of the Gravel Garden, with ducks paddling through the ponds; water lilies and giant rhubarb, little bridges and a stream lined with ferns,

Left The Water Garden features four ponds with water lilies and colourful marginal planting.

Opposite The Gravel Garden with ornamental grasses, sage, penstemon and verbena in late summer.

marsh marigolds and candelabra primulas, and a long walk under oak trees lined with impressive displays of shade-tolerant plants.

The Reservoir Garden further along has beds of tall, late-season perennials and grasses, while the Scree Garden by the house is a different kind of dry garden, to mimic the side of a mountain, with raised beds of alpine plants. The Woodland Garden was created out of the wreckage of the Great Storm of 1987, and is at its best in spring with snowdrops, hellebores and daffodils, as well as woodland treasures like erythroniums and trilliums.

Since Beth's death in 2018, her family and the garden team continue to manage and develop the garden, based on her principles. They don't feed plants and irrigate very little, and never in the Gravel Garden. All the materials used, such as gravel and sand, are sourced locally, and they mulch with recycled green waste from the local council. The nursery is peat free, and efforts are made to reduce the amount of plastic that leaves the site – if you buy a plant, you can take it out of the pot at the till or bring it back later to be reused.

Beth wrote several influential books and was passionate about educating people on sustainability. A true trailblazer, her ideas and garden have informed and inspired so many, including top international gardeners and designers, who carry on her work in their own way in gardens around the world.

PROSPECT COTTAGE, KENT

On the edge of a desolate headland on the Kent coast, on a stark shingle beach, by the hulking grey bulk of a nuclear power station, sits a small pitch-stained cottage with an extraordinary wild garden. It was created by the painter, theatre designer, film director and writer Derek Jarman in the late 1980s, and remains one of his most endearing works – a piece of site-sensitive art that could not be more of its place.

He discovered Prospect Cottage by chance in 1986, while visiting the distinctive hamlet of Dungeness. The little black fisherman's shack was set in a surreal landscape that many find bleak, barren and eerie, like a vision of a post-apocalyptic world.

But the vast skies and unlimited views out to sea offered by the broad, flat terrain, and the remarkable features of the power station and lighthouse, scattering of huts and forgotten fishing boats, spoke to Derek. He had just been diagnosed with HIV, and the cottage and the garden he made here became his refuge as he dealt with this and the AIDS-related illness that followed.

It was here that he wrote the book *Modern Nature*, and filmed *The Garden*, inspired by the creation of the garden and the connection he felt with the land and nature. He faced some extremely challenging conditions – salty winds that erode every

surface and scour all but the very toughest vegetation, and baking sun that bleaches whatever remains.

Dungeness was a private estate, and the owner forbade residents to erect boundaries, which meant no fences or walls could be built to protect garden plants. This limitation of no limits is, however, what makes this space so special, as it flows out and merges with ease into the surrounding natural landscape, making it seem as if the whole beach is the garden.

The headland is an important ecological site, a Special Area of Conservation and a National Nature Reserve, with, despite appearances, an incredible range of fauna and flora. Derek took his cue from the indigenous plants that manage to survive in the shingle, and planted drought- and salt-tolerant natives like sea kale, and Mediterranean plants like lavender, santolina and sedums.

Derek died in 1994, but the garden is still very much how he made it. The odd grass toughs it out with bright and colourful self-seeders like red poppies. The beds have borders of white beach stone, and dotted throughout there are eye-catching sculptures made from driftwood and rusty metal objects he found on the shore. The poem 'The Sun Rising' by John Donne adorns the wall at the side of the cottage.

A fundraising campaign in 2020 has ensured that Prospect Cottage and its garden stay safe from sale or development, and will be managed by a local organisation as an arts residency.

Below Mien Ruys was ahead of her time in her modern, experimental approach to planting and design in her garden in the Netherlands.

A POTTED HISTORY OF MODERN NATURALISTIC PLANTING

The history of the naturalistic planting style is an intriguing chain of influences, inspirations, mentorships and connections between various people on both sides of the Atlantic.

William Robinson's *The English Flower Garden* had far more impact during his lifetime than his book *The Wild Garden* did, but his ideas spurred on his friend Gertrude Jekyll. Although she is best known for her colour-theory herbaceous borders, she also developed an enduring style of woodland planting that perfectly suited England's climate and habitat conditions.

Their work excited a young nurseryman in the Netherlands, called Bonne Ruys, who founded the Moerheim nursery and successfully bred many border perennials, which then became popular in England in the early 1900s. Around the same time, in Germany, a nurseryman named Karl Foerster was also experimenting with plant breeding, focusing on colourful cold-hardy perennials and ornamental grasses, introducing 400 new varieties to market, including *Rudbeckia fulgida* var. *sullivantii* 'Goldsturm'. In the 1930s, he found a grass seedling in the Hamburg Botanic Garden by chance and named it after himself. *Calamagrostis* x *acutiflora* 'Karl Foerster', with its vertical habit and long season, remains a stalwart plant for naturalistic schemes.

He mentored another young plantsman, Ernst Pagels, who took up the baton and went on to breed many of the *Miscanthus* grass varieties in cultivation today, as well as the popular *Salvia nemorosa* 'Ostfriesland'. These were the men who created the plants that made everything that came next possible.

Back in the Netherlands, between the wars, Bonne Ruys' daughter Mien took over the design department of the business. Through much experimentation, failure and success with planting, she realised it was best to choose the plants that suited the situation, rather than changing the soil. There was no education available in 'garden architecture' or landscape design in the Netherlands, so she trained in England and Germany, and got involved with the 'Delft school' of architecture, attending lectures in Amsterdam. She decided on an architectural style with loose planting.

Her ideas and own experimental garden had an enormous impact on Henk Gerritsen, a Dutch biology teacher and gardener who liked to travel to see plants in the wild. He used Ruys' principle of 'wild planting in a strong design' when developing his garden, Priona, but struggled to find the plants he wanted, that were tough enough to outcompete weeds but had a natural feel. He found some at the small nursery of a young Piet Oudolf, and the two men began a friendship and working relationship that produced several mould-breaking books on naturalistic plants.

They were two of the main founders of what became known as the Dutch Wave, New Wave or

Left The Oudolf Field at the Hauser & Wirth gallery in Somerset, in the modern naturalistic planting style.

New Perennial Movement. Before this, the pinnacle of style had been the English garden with neat strips of border filled with obviously designed, high-maintenance mixed planting – tall shrubs at the back, blocks of various perennials in the middle, low things at the front – where highly bred flowers were prized for big, heavy, colourful blooms, everything peaked around June and was cut down in autumn.

The new style instead created meadow-like swathes where plants were arranged in drifts. The displays tended to peak in July and continue on into autumn, and they were left up until the following spring. The shape of the plant – whether it was a spire or globe or wispy in form – and how it died back and kept its structure over winter were just as important, if not more so, than the colour. Everything was planted densely, so staking was not required. The plants used were often those bred by European nurserymen like Foerster and Pagels from originally North American grassland species of perennials and tall ornamental grasses – leading to this style also being called 'prairie planting'.

Foerster had also mentored a gardener and landscape architect called Wolfgang Oehme, who moved to the US in 1957. In the 1970s, he joined forces with James van Sweden, an American-Dutch landscape architect who had studied at Delft, just like Mien Ruys. Van Sweden was greatly influenced by Ruys' approach and by his professor, Jan Bijhouwer, who believed that you should make a garden solid with plants, like a meadow, and then

wherever people walked you created paths – but you didn't design the paths until the people showed you where the paths should be. Together, Oehme and Van Sweden promoted the New American Garden, a tapestry-style arrangement of North American perennials and grasses that had much in common with the Dutch Wave, but had a more ecological bent in using many native species.

This new form took the gardening world by storm. Oudolf had a particularly aesthetic and painterly approach and, with public projects such as the Lurie Garden in Chicago and the High Line in New York, has become an international superstar. In fact, as naturalistic planting has continued to evolve, it has developed most in regard to public spaces like urban parks, to bring nature into the city for people and wildlife in the most high-impact but low-input ways possible.

Cassian Schmidt, who spent time with Oehme, Van Sweden and their nurserymen in America, has been doing trials and maintenance experiments at Hermannshof Gardens in Germany since the late 1990s to help create best practice for sustainable municipal schemes. In the UK, professors Nigel Dunnett and James Hitchmough of the Department of Landscape Architecture at the University of Sheffield, founders of what is known as the 'Sheffield School' of planting design, have focused on colourful, stylised 'wild' plantings to delight, for example, visitors to the Olympic Park in London, or the residents of the capital's Barbican estate. Their inspirations are usually natural plant communities, 'enhanced' into dynamic mixes of native and non-native plants, blended in a pattern that mimics how things grow in the wild. Hitchmough specialises in seed mixes, while Dunnett likes to layer up with shrubs as well as bulbs and perennials. In the US, along a similar vein, landscape architect Thomas Rainer is advocating for ecological aesthetics –

beautiful, biodiverse, low-maintenance landscapes that bring the natural world into the urban realm.

Until now, the main innovators have been nurserymen producing new plants, and designers using those plants to create interpretations of wild habitats. However, with the difficulties presented by our changing climate, in the future it may be experimental gardeners who forge our next course, doing seemingly unnatural things, like earth moving and growing in sand, in the name of naturalism. Some of the most exciting are Peter Korn, a Swedish gardener-plantsman who grows in pure sand, creating naturalistic gardens in Eskilsby and Klinta, and John Little of Hilldrop in Essex, who is experimenting with growing in recycled crushed concrete and ceramics. Perhaps the next revolution will not be about what we grow, but what we grow it in.

WALTHAM PLACE, BERKSHIRE

Henk Gerritsen described his style at Priona Gardens in the Netherlands as 'dreamt nature' – a beautifully evocative description – though others might call it managed chaos. Creating a natural garden here from the late 1970s, he adopted Mien Ruys' ethos of wild planting in a strong design, and then pushed it as far as it would go.

There was a solid background structure, and playful topiary, with planting that combined garden plants, wild species and thuggish weeds. Instead of constantly battling the most pernicious invaders, Henk used natural-looking, strong-growing plants to outcompete them or at least control their spread. The entire life cycle of plants from fresh spring leaves to decaying winter stalks was appreciated. No chemical fertilisers or pesticides were used, and he was pragmatic and accepting of pests and diseases. The results were a step too far for many gardeners, but others embraced his experimental ideas and his wish to join forces with rather than fight nature.

When Strilli Oppenheimer visited in 1999, she knew she had found a kindred soul, and asked Henk to redesign her gardens at Waltham Place in Berkshire along the same lines. Waltham, a 220-acre estate, comprised an ancient farm, woodlands and formal ornamental areas that had been redesigned in the early 20th century. Strilli's husband, Nikki

Oppenheimer, inherited it in 1984, and the couple converted the whole estate to organic growing, and then biodynamics.

Henk kept the 17th-century walled garden layout and Edwardian-era features, and worked within this design. The Square Garden has retained its pool and central Italianate pergola walk, which froths over with white roses in summer. Henk's whimsy is shown in the clipped 'caterpillar' of box hedging that runs from one side of the garden to the other. Ground elder, usually the bane of gardeners' lives, but beloved here for its long season of white umbelliferous flowers, is kept somewhat

at bay behind this boundary by robust growers such as *Persicaria polymorpha* and *Calamagrostis* x *acutiflora* 'Karl Foerster'. On the opposite side, a self-sown river of *Stipa tenuissima* has completely obscured what was once a path.

A small Butterfly Garden has a path that spirals inward through carefree plantings of airy pimpinella, marjoram and mallow, while the Friar's Walk alongside is lined with fine shrubs like *Garrya* and interesting grasses and perennials. There is a Potager with perennial vegetables like asparagus and rhubarb, and a riot of flowers, wild, self-seeded and cultivated, like a cutting garden gone rogue.

Opposite The Long Border is cleverly structured with intermittent curves of beech hedging infilled with grasses.

Right A red admiral butterfly sips nectar from blooms of red valerian at Waltham Place.

Outside the walls is an orchard with old trees strewn with roses, as well as a large woodland and a lake, where the bats swoop gracefully in a nightly ballet. One of Henk's experiments here was the New Garden, a wet meadow habitat alive with crickets, where mown paths thread around sections of scrubby wild flowers and long grass that have been marked out with deep edging.

In front of the house, the 70-metre double Long Border is the perfect expression of Henk's design ideals. He clipped the backdrop yew hedging into loose cloud forms and added semi-circles of low beech hedging to break up the length, infilled with blocks of *Anemanthele lessoniana*. There are still herbaceous perennials, but they are joined by ornamental grasses like *Miscanthus* and *Pennisetum*, and wild plants like burdock and hemlock. The garden team do take out nettles and thistles, but leave bindweed. On Strilli's urging, Henk tried to grow this white-trumpet-flowered climber – one of the perennial weeds most dreaded by gardeners – politely over border obelisks, but it refused, preferring to scramble over the hedges, and so it continues to do so.

The gardeners constantly strive to find the balance between letting things go completely wild and maintaining some sense of order. The hedges

are trimmed and the paths weeded, so there is
still some formality, but otherwise there is little
intervention. The planting is solid and close-knit,
almost impenetrable, with the most competitive
species and cultivars having long ago won out over
more diminutive and delicate specimens. Things
self-seed with gusto, but if plants die off, they are not
replaced. Whatever stays in the garden has to be able
to cope with the rough and tumble.

It's all part of the Waltham aim to create an
environment that is self-sustaining, a closed cycle:
nothing comes into the garden and nothing goes
out. Everything is composted, and everything
gets mulched. In the productive areas such as the
vegetable garden, seed is saved, and damage from
pests and diseases is limited by crop rotation,
companion planting, green manures and biodynamic
preparations made from home-grown nettles,
comfrey and horsetail. Microorganisms are even
harvested from the woods. All the different areas of
the estate support each other, and the ornamental
gardens contribute by drawing in beneficial insects.
Wildlife surveys have revealed an array of butterflies
and moths, as well as over 50 species of bee.

The garden may seem unruly and unkempt to
some visitors, challenging their preconceptions of
what a garden should look like, and what plants
deserve their place. It is radical, and a confronting
experience, but perhaps one that could alter
entrenched perspectives and ultimately prove
inspiring and liberating for wild gardeners.

WILDSIDE, DEVON

You will not find a more innovative garden-maker than Keith Wiley, or a more exciting garden than Wildside. On first viewing, it's intense. The striking topography, massed technicoloured planting and intricate layering of forms and textures leaves the visitor reeling pleasantly from visual overload, mouth agape. You have never seen anything quite like this.

The scale of Keith's plans is ambitious – 'borderline madness,' he says. He was head gardener at The Garden House, on the edge of Dartmoor, for many years before he and his wife Ros decided to set up on their own, buying 3 acres of field down the road in 2004. The intention was to make a new garden and nursery, but their method was bold and the results dramatic.

Instead of seizing a shovel, Keith got a mini-digger, and moved tonnes upon tonnes of earth, completely reshaping and transforming the flat pasture into an extraordinary undulating landscape of hills and valleys. These mounds and banks were then covered with a diverse selection of closely packed planting, the like of which has never been seen in the wild, but which was entirely inspired by it.

Keith looked at how plants grow in the wild – into and through each other instead of in blocks – and paid attention to the conditions that they grew in, but beyond this, he had no interest in replicating actual natural communities. Instead, plants from all across the world that would never meet in the wild, but enjoy the same sorts of situations, hang out happily. It's right plant, right place – it's just that rather than working with the habitat that was there, Keith created his own.

Despite all the earth sculpting and arch-curation, the effect is soothingly naturalistic. 'It's about creating the feeling that you get when you see the flowers in the wild,' Keith explains. 'It's subconscious, tapping into memories of places. It's idealised nature – you won't find anywhere like this in nature, but it's capturing the spirit of a place in the wild.' He loved the look and mood of ancient olive groves, for example, but knew olive trees would grow too slowly at Wildside, so used a brace of silver-leaved *Elaeagnus* to get the same effect.

The first area to be completed is behind the house. Narrow grit paths cut through the swathes of planting, snaking this way and that, giving you a choice of routes to follow. Repeated acers, magnolias and choice conifers break up tracts of energetic perennials and airy grasses, rising up on sunny banks all around to immerse you completely in the planting. Shady corners feature artfully contrasting

foliage plants. There's a small orchard meadow, and a lush Water Garden, its ponds framed with intermingling moisture-loving plants.

On the other side of the house is the Courtyard Garden, framed all round with a wisteria pergola, and punctuated by tall-trunked cordylines that stretch up above raised beds of drought-tolerant planting. 'It's a little bit of New Mexico, South Africa and the Mediterranean all jumbled together, like putting them in a blender and coming out with a smoothie,' Keith says. He is a gardening magpie, taking a little bit of this and a little bit of that from various places, an effect or style or plant or feature he has seen – the colour of the walls at the far end mimics the pink sandstone cliffs of Bryce Canyon National Park, Utah.

In the Canyons area, a large hill is smothered in vibrant vegetation, with 100 different types of agapanthus in shades of blue, and crocosmias and day lilies in soft oranges and yellows through July and August. The swaying ornamental grasses in between give a wonderful sense of movement.

Next to this is Keith's last area to develop – a tribute garden for Ros, who died in 2019. It is his most ambitious design to date, looking to capture the essence of magnificent wild flower displays he had seen in South Africa. He has carved up the earth to create towering banks 7.5 metres higher than the original ground level, mounding deep sand beds and covering them with shale. Birch trees and conifers create a naturalistic backdrop in what now appears, intentionally, rather like a disused quarry. Waterfalls

Left Keith has sculpted the
site into valleys smothered in
naturalistic planting, including
Erigeron daisies.

Opposite The garden
is influenced by, but not
attempting to emulate,
natural landscapes from
around the world.

tumble down the slopes to crystal clear ponds, reflecting the masses of flowering bulbs and South African plants that explode out of the stony ground with flamboyant seasonal colour. It has a completely different mood and planting to the lower garden, the Courtyard or the Canyons Bank, but it's created on the same principles. As Keith puts it, 'It's the same ideas, just different personnel.'

His innovative approach also sees him shaping plants in unusual ways, raising the crowns of trees to show off the bark and create views through the branches, or letting wisteria grow like a shrub rather than training it as a climber. Of course, these experiments and his garden-design gambles are rooted in his deep horticultural knowledge – he knows all the rules, so he can break them. But they are also borne out of an even deeper belief in what he is doing. The garden is stunning, but Keith's vision for it is staggering. 'You can learn lessons from what you see in the wild,' he says. 'We could be on the verge of something absolutely amazing in gardening if we looked to nature and learned from it.'

THE BARN GARDEN PRAIRIE, HERTFORDSHIRE

Garden designer Tom Stuart-Smith has created a host of prestigious projects, but one of his most loved is his own home garden in Hertfordshire. Made over many years, what was once an arable field is now a formal contemporary-style courtyard and a wider garden of hedged compartments with lawns and borders, as well as wildflower meadows.

Inspired by the late-summer splendour of the natural grasslands of North America, Tom decided to create his own prairie here in almost an acre of goat paddock in 2011. It's an eye-popping, jaw-dropping, slightly overwhelming experience to walk among the kaleidoscopically colourful planting, some of which reaches up, up above your head to 3 metres tall. 'It is a bit bonkers,' he says. 'When people see it, it is such unfamiliar stuff, it makes you recalibrate what plants look like.'

This was always meant to be an experiment ground. Tom had worked on several prairie planting schemes for clients before, but some had not performed or lasted well due to maintenance issues or unsuccessful plant relationships. 'I wanted to look after it myself, to see how predictable and unpredictable it was, and how it developed over a period of time,' he explains.

Rather than using plants or plugs, the planting was created through seed mixes designed by Professor James Hitchmough of the Sheffield School. Prairies are intricate ecosystems of native North American herbaceous perennials and grasses, which grow very densely – 100 plants per square metre or more, rather than the typical seven or eight per metre in a normal border. Sowing the scheme meant that the plants could all grow and develop together as a community, in as spontaneous a way as possible. 'I love the fact that there's this sort of in-built alchemy in doing everything from seed,' says Tom.

Hitchmough tailored bespoke mixes to suit the mainly dry, free-draining soil conditions and one damper area of heavy clay. The resulting package of seed – no bigger than a bag of sugar but worth thousands of pounds – contained about 45 different species and selections.

To prepare the space, a hedge was planted around it, and a fence was put up to keep out rabbits and other animals. The existing scrubby grass was sprayed with herbicide, and then the earth was turned and levelled with a digger, before large sinuous beds were marked out and covered with about 75mm of sand. Tom and his helpers mixed the

seed with sawdust and sowed directly into the sand on a calm, wind-free day, scattering by hand for a natural, random effect. Then the beds were covered in jute mesh to keep the birds off and the seed in, and regularly watered to encourage germination.

The first year was challenging, with an enormous amount of hand weeding, as endless buttercups were brought up in the casts of earthworms, and unwanted willows sprouted out of the sand. With such an unusual, unknown planting palette, it wasn't easy to identify seedlings, and it's likely that some planned plants that never appeared, such as *Andropogon* and *Sorghastrum* grasses, were meticulously weeded out by accident at this time in the mistaken belief that they were couch or lawn grass.

But over the following seasons, the planting got better and better, and in the intervening decade it has evolved. Some plants stuck around for the first few years but are now scarce or absent, while others tend to dominate. 'Stoloniferous asters will take over the world,' Tom says, only half joking. He has added things – 'I haven't been very purist about it' – including shrubs like *Rhus* and South African perennials; around 15–20 new species in all.

In spring and early summer, the space begins to green and the first spots of colour come from hot pink *Dianthus carthusianorum* and *Echinacea pallida*. It really gets going in midsummer with rods of mauve *Liatris pycnostachya* and architectural silver *Eryngium agavifolium*. Flowering reaches a peak in August and continues into autumn, featuring *Euphorbia corollata*, galtonias, big *Silphium terebinthimaceum* and *S. laciniatum*, coreopsis, rudbeckia, asters and red-hot pokers.

Although the scheme is elaborate and its establishment was involved, ongoing maintenance is not. Everything gets left up over winter, and strimmed down to the ground in February. There's no staking, as the plants are so tightly packed that they support each other. There's no need to feed, and no watering unless there happens to be a drought. 'It's a different way of managing a piece of land – not gardening in the usual sense of the word, more vegetation management. Maintenance is about halfway between a border and a native meadow.'

Originally described as a heightened interpretation of a prairie, it has developed into what Tom now feels more comfortable calling an exotic meadow. 'It's pretty hyper for a prairie,' he says. 'There probably aren't any natural prairies that are quite as floriferous as this.'

MEADOWS

Wildflower meadows are vital, species-rich habitats for wildlife. The native wild flowers that grow in these semi-natural landscapes provide sustenance for many insects, which are in turn a food source for birds and small mammals, which then become food for much larger animals.

These relationships developed over hundreds of years, in symbiosis with farmers' traditional methods of managing their fields of hay, creating a perfectly adapted ecosystem. However, due to modern industrial agricultural practices, urbanisation and changes in land management in the UK, we have lost more than 97 per cent of our meadows since the Second World War.

'Meadow' is a term that has been bandied around a lot in recent years by gardeners, to the point that it has become confused and misunderstood. A true wildflower meadow will contain native wild grassland plants such as bird's foot trefoil, selfheal, orchids, cowslips, ox-eye daisies, cuckoo flower, harebell and knapweed, among others, depending on the soil and situation. Cornfield annuals like field poppies and cornflowers, which feature in packets of sold 'wildflower meadow' seed mix, are not meadow plants, but are popular for sowing a swath of colourful annual flowers that bloom for a few months in summer.

This idea has been developed further into a naturalistic style of mass planting, called pictorial meadows, which mixes perennial and annual natives and non-natives to create an idealised meadow-like effect. There are many excellent attributes to this style of planting, which is more suited to the rich, fertile earth of gardens than the impoverished soil required for real meadows. It does, however, contribute to some muddying of public understanding for those trying to conserve real meadows, and the native British wild flowers which are so important for wildlife.

Some landowners are embracing the opportunity to turn pastures and fields back to meadow, or create a new meadow from scratch. Whole rolls of wildflower turf, grown by specialist companies, are available, as are bespoke seed mixes. To do it this way, the top layer of vegetation must be removed

To prevent strong-growing grasses from outcompeting everything else, meadow makers use a plant called yellow rattle, a hemiparasitic annual. It feeds off the roots of grasses, which reduces their vigour, leaving space for more delicate flowers to come through.

Meadows follow an annual cycle. They are left to grow and flower in spring and summer, so the plants set seed, before being cut down between midsummer and early autumn. Traditionally this was done by hand with a scythe, and this method has had a revival, especially since lighter, easier-to-use Austrian scythes became available. Hand cutting gives wildlife a better chance of surviving the cut and also improves seed setting success rates. Once set, the cuttings are eaten by grazing animals or removed to keep the fertility of the soil down.

Naturally attractive to plant-loving gardeners, meadows require a larger amount of land than the typical UK garden. Although gardens could never substitute for the loss of 7.5 million acres of meadow, a wildflower patch within the garden is a great way to develop an affinity for and deeper understanding of these special habitats. If using a seed mix, try to choose one with native British wild flowers appropriate to your conditions and area, and make sure to source from a reputable supplier.

first. Although this can be done mechanically, often the area is cleared by spraying with herbicide – an approach that conflicts with the objectives of enhancing biodiversity and sustainability.

If possible, it is preferable to let natural vegetation regenerate, or to transfer fresh-cut hay from another meadow in the area to introduce the seed of flora with local provenance – plants to which the local wildlife is already adapted.

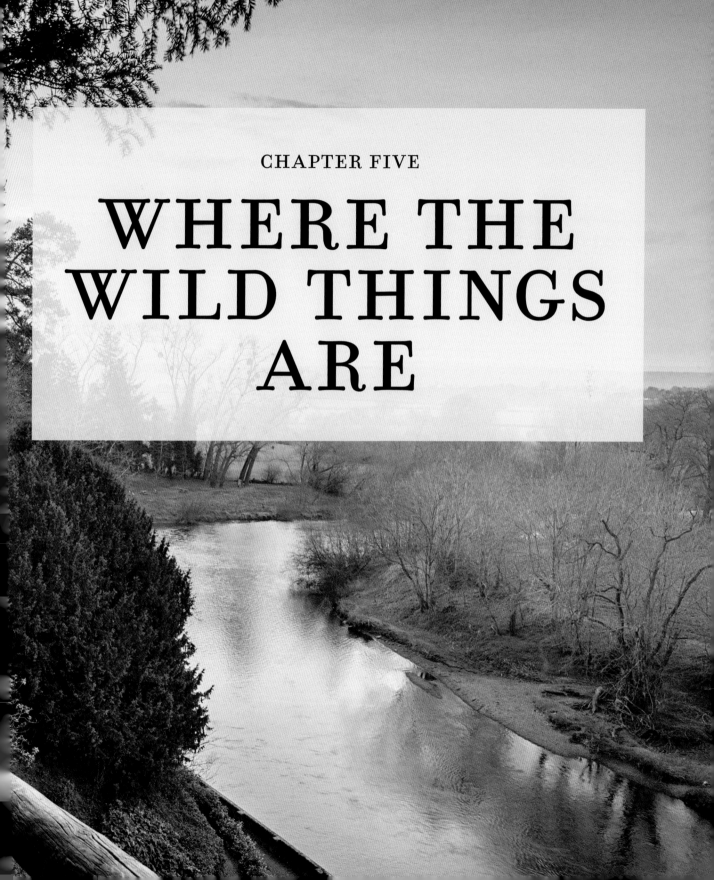

CHAPTER FIVE

WHERE THE WILD THINGS ARE

Get back to nature at these fantastic places that focus on attracting, protecting and conserving wildlife, creating homes and habitats for a whole host of butterflies, birds, furry creatures and creepy-crawlies.

COLBY WOODLAND GARDEN, PEMBROKESHIRE

A few minutes' walk from the sea in south-west Wales, this 30-acre garden lies in an open grassy valley framed on both sides by wooded hills. It is a haven for wildlife and actively managed to provide a chain of joined-up habitats throughout the garden and the wider farmland and estate.

It wasn't always so idyllic. The wildflower meadow in front of the house, with its burbling stream, looks like it has been here forever, but this area was once an industrial landscape pockmarked by mineshafts and spoil heaps. The woods, which are now the ideal place to get in touch with nature, were planted for timber. These money-making schemes dried up after the Industrial Revolution, and Colby became a seaside holiday home for well-off Victorians who turned these scarred grounds into a garden.

The Walled Garden with its ornate octagonal gazebo, rill and flower beds, may date from this time, but even here, in the most designed, cultivated part of the garden, everything is managed for biodiversity, and chemicals are not used to control pests and diseases.

Gardening at Colby is all about creating overlapping habitats for a variety of interdependent species. In summer, the 4-acre flood meadow is left to grow long, creating an abundant wildflower display that draws in bees, butterflies and other important pollinators. Its streams and ponds attract dragonflies, damselflies and other insects, which attract fish such as trout, which in turn attract otters. The sheltered wetland area at the bottom is a helpful habitat for amphibians such as frogs, toads and newts, and these creatures entice grass snakes, which nest and bask nearby. The otters use the area to teach their cubs to swim.

Almost half of the woodland of Colby is native oak, the most species-rich habitat in the country, and at least 45 species of breeding birds, including the wood warbler and the pied flycatcher, have been seen here. The woodland also supports a vast array of invertebrates, which provide food for birds like firecrests, nuthatches and treecreepers, and small mammals like dormice. They in turn provide food for the garden's birds of prey, which include buzzards, red kites, barn and tawny owls, goshawks and sparrowhawks.

In the East Wood, there are glades of beech, plane, pine and larch trees, and a growing collection

Previous page The bridge at the top of
The Weir Garden, Herefordshire, gives
far-reaching views over the River Wye
and its banks.

Below An adventure awaits
along the winding paths
through the grounds of
Colby Woodland Garden.

of Japanese maples, including some unusual varieties, as well as a small grove of wild service trees, *Sorbus torminalis*. On the opposite side, the West Wood has more intriguing finds, including the tallest Japanese cedar in the UK.

Interesting pieces from the garden's mining heritage, and unusual monuments from artistic past owners, hide in among the trees, as do the prized rhododendrons that thrive in the valley's acidic soil and fill the pathways with colour in May and June. In spring, there are swathes of bluebells too, while in summer, hydrangeas take over the show.

Here and there a dead tree trunk has been left to rot down rather than being cleared away. This is an important part of the conservation strategy. Standing deadwood creates a home for the garden's bats, woodpeckers and beetles. Lying deadwood is perfect for fungi, and at Colby they can boast to having rare chicken-of-the-woods mushrooms

(*Laetiporus sulphureus*), horse's hoof fungus (*Fomes fomentarius*) and King Alfred's cakes (*Daldinia concentrica*). In the wider estate, meadows have been sown with wildflower seed or developed naturally, and farmland is being left with wide field margins and shaggy hedgerows to create wildlife corridors that connect the east and west woodland.

It's an excellent habitat for humans too, especially those young and young at heart. Wild play is encouraged with a range of elements and activities, from pond dipping and playing pooh-sticks, to making a dam or mud pies. Daring adventurers can take a turn on the rope swing or climb the large fallen tree trunk in the meadow, while explorers can search for the den in the bamboo grove, or the secret fairy doors and hidden hedge house in the woods. It is the perfect place for all creatures great and small to run wild.

WILD PLAY

There is growing concern that children growing up in our digital and increasingly urbanised society are less connected to nature than previous generations, and are missing out and even suffering as a result. It's been dubbed 'Nature Deficit Disorder' – 'what happens when people, particularly children, spend little or no time outside in natural environments, resulting in physical and mental problems, including anxiety and distraction', according to author Richard Louv.

However, just because these modern children spend less time outside in nature, it does not follow that they enjoy it any less than their parents or grandparents did while young. Much of children's leisure time is now spent on screens or in adult-created activities such as organised sports, but it has been shown that frequent, make-it-up-as-you-go-along style play outdoors is beneficial in a multitude of ways, boosting their physical, cognitive, creative, emotional and social development.

To reap the most benefits, this unstructured, child-centred play should be with the elements of nature and not just happen to be in nature or outdoors (such as an artificial playground). This is the reason why forest schools and wild play areas in gardens and woodlands have begun to spring up in recent years.

The main ingredients required are the space and ability for kids to explore at their own pace. The optimum habitat is a simple little patch of rough ground where they can dig in the mud, build a den out of sticks or climb things. Wild play offers the chance to gauge risk and feel the thrill of mild peril, to observe wildlife or collect leaves or rocks, or just suddenly forget all that on a whim and jump in a puddle or stream.

What is important is that the child decides what they want to do and for how long. They don't mind if it's raining or they get dirty – it's part of the fun. All you have to do is regularly bring them to a natural space where they can be adventurous, experiment and try things.

Regular sessions of this sort of play throughout the seasons won't just benefit the kids. These nature or wild play experiences have been shown to have a powerful effect on people's concern for

the environment in later life – in fact, they are the most important element in fostering an ongoing relationship with the natural world and a wish to conserve it as an adult.

This is particularly important when it comes to plants. 'Plant blindness' is a term that was coined to describe people's inability to see or notice plants in their environment, which results in an underappreciation of plants. The less exposure children get to plants, the more plant blind they become. This could be disastrous to efforts to conserve endangered flora – if large charismatic mammals such as tigers and pandas are in trouble,

the chances of saving a rare orchid or tree nobody notices or cares about are slim. You have to see it to save it.

However, as the song goes, the children are our future, and increasing the frequency and variety of ways they see and interact with plants will reduce plant blindness. Whether it is through gardening, foraging, wild walks, visiting landscapes like the gardens in this book, or a combination of all of these things, it will help. It's up to you, because the second most common influence in kids forming a lasting bond with nature, after regular wild play, is encouragement from adults who share a love of nature.

Above left Time spent in touch with nature will help children to appreciate the living world.

Above There are lots of options for wild play.

Right Running free outdoors is good for everyone's health and happiness.

133

THE WEIR GARDEN, HEREFORDSHIRE

On a bend of the River Wye lies The Weir, an unusual, almost secret garden that clings to the steep slopes above the river bank. Originally a Georgian pleasure ground, it is blessed with a range of habitats from woodland to water and sun-baked hillside, in which a multitude of wildlife has been given licence to live and roam. Roger Parr, a banker from Manchester, bought it in the 1920s and began developing the bones of the 10-acre garden we see now, creating walks below the house by cutting paths across the slopes.

The Weir is known predominantly as a spring garden, with fantastic displays of flowering bulbs from February on, including masses of snowdrops and daffodils, but also fritillaries, scillas, bluebells and camassias, which are joined by primroses, violets and ransoms. These early blooms are a welcome nectar source for pollinators.

Parr's companion Victor Morris lived in the mansion until his death in 1985, but the garden had been neglected for some years before this. When Ned Price became head gardener in 1987, it was completely overgrown, but he recognised that this had attracted a range of wildlife, and decided to manage the garden minimally, with nature in mind.

This was a bold move at a time when wild flowers were considered unwelcome weeds and the idea of 'rewilding' an as yet untried experiment.

Advocates of wildlife gardening found it difficult to persuade a nation of lawn-loving, hedges-and-edges gardeners that messy could be marvellous, and many visitors were not fans of Ned's 'let it be, wait and see' approach – but the birds, bees and butterflies certainly were.

More than 70 types of bird have been recorded in the garden's biannual surveys in summer and winter, including finches and warblers, robins and martins, woodpeckers, swifts and swallows, thrushes and red wings, their names like poetry to the birdwatchers who use the garden's bird hide. Glimpsed on the river are kingfishers, egrets, oystercatchers and linnets. There are also bats, including Brandt's bats and whiskered bats, a host of bees, butterflies and moths, and turquoise clouds of damselflies by the water.

Ned retired after 31 years here, but his ethos has been carried on, with plants permitted to escape and self-seed where they choose, popping up unexpectedly in a pretty, random manner.

The bridge that traverses the precipice at the top of the garden is a literally breathtaking introduction to the terrain and outlook, but this dramatic opening view soon disappears as you enter the dark and mysterious woodland. Further down, by the river's edge, fish can be observed swimming in the shallows. The waterside location is both a boon and a challenge – up to 2 metres of the garden can be lost to the river in one winter through erosion, and the floods can damage trees. The river bank is a designated Site of Special Scientific Interest, however, and is also home to great crested newts, swans and ducks, and otters, who leave their telltale footprints in the boathouse.

The open hillside that stretches along the river bank was once a more formal, ornamental garden,

and some of the topiary from this time survives. These large, clipped, bulbous shapes, reminiscent of buns or mushrooms, are now surrounded not by well-behaved herbaceous perennials but by grass left to grow long all summer, and this wild sward is packed with mostly native flowers, which have been allowed to find their own space. Pale yellow evening primrose, spiky teasels and mulleins wave in the gentle breeze, with a flurry of purple-blue campanulas, bursts of poppies, hemp agrimony and red campion. Brambles make up ground beside valerian, purple loosestrife, wild marjoram, ox-eye daisies and knapweed, and there are occasional discoveries that speak of a more cultivated past, like a glorious tree peony.

This diverse range of plants is perfect for attracting a wide range of wildlife, and much of it is left up over winter to offer shelter and food for birds and small mammals. The 'live and let live' motto has to be suspended, however, when it comes to several invasive plants, including Japanese knotweed, that wash in off the river, as the garden team is legally obliged to control them so they don't spread to nearby land.

Further along, a restored walled garden is an altogether more organised space, with lines of fruit and a beautiful glasshouse. But even here, in this paragon of order, things spill over freely and are allowed to seed into the paths.

Opposite Beautiful mature trees are a feature throughout the garden and contribute much to supporting the diverse wildlife.

Right The Weir is known for its spring bulb displays, including native, moisture-loving meadow plants like snakeshead fritillaries.

Left Boost wellbeing with a walk in the woods, such as Janet's Foss at Malham Tarn Estate in Yorkshire.

NATURE THERAPY

In his book *Biophilia*, biologist Edward O. Wilson introduced the idea that humans have an innate connection with and affinity for nature, 'the urge to affiliate with other forms of life'. It's what draws us to plants and animals, and why, it seems, we feel better around them.

Studies at the University of Derby found that improving a person's connection with nature led to significant increases in their well-being. As well as this, there is a growing body of work linking access to nature with positive mental health outcomes, such as significant reductions in depression and anxiety.

In the 1980s, the Japanese government conducted research into these effects, asking participants to spend two hours of mindful exploration in a forest. The results showed this activity could boost their immune systems, reduce blood pressure, lower the level of stress hormone, and improve concentration and memory. 'Shinrin-yoku', or forest bathing, was launched as a national health programme.

This activity does not require a swimsuit, as it has nothing to do with water – it is simply about being immersed among the trees, observing nature. To give it a try, find a quiet woodland (there are many looked after by the National Trust and the Woodland Trust). Once there, turn off your phone, and try to clear your mind. Walk slowly, and breathe deeply. Use all your senses to take in the smell of the forest, the sound of birds, the colours of the leaves. Be in the place, and in the moment.

141

If you can't get to a forest, try a park for your nature fix – one Asian study found that students who walked in a park for 15 minutes in autumn had decreased stress and heart rates. These sorts of beneficial effects are now being further explored and used as a means of preventing or easing ill health, in a set of practices known as nature therapy. Green prescribing is seen increasingly as a potential tool, with GPs being asked to consider getting patients to exercise outdoors in natural and green spaces as part of their treatments on the 'Natural Health Service'.

Most of the evidence available is on green spaces generally, with little specific data on the impact of gardens and gardening on health, but anyone who has lugged around a watering can, weeded a border or dug a planting hole can attest to the physical exertion and fitness level that gardening requires. Aside from being a good way to stay fit, advocates see gardens as intrinsically therapeutic and healing environments that can help support recovery from illness, with charities such as Horatio's Garden and Maggie's Centres providing beautiful outdoor spaces around hospitals and cancer care centres. The effects of gardens in care homes have been well studied, showing that time in a garden can reduce agitation and aggression in dementia sufferers, and improve their concentration and memory recall. There is also research being done on the contribution of community food growing to both physical and mental health.

Living in greener areas is associated with lower levels of mental distress and higher well-being, while living more than a mile away from green spaces increases the likelihood of people reporting high levels of stress by 40 per cent. We need more, better designed, randomised controlled studies to gain a deeper understanding of how green spaces affect us and why, for behind these findings there are certainly more complex causal factors to consider, such as socio-economic inequalities. A major challenge for many people is the availability of and access to good-quality, nearby green space.

If we are all to benefit from the health advantages our gardens, parks and natural spaces can provide, we must conserve these places not just as homes for plants and wildlife, but as important habitats for us humans too.

143

FYNE COURT, SOMERSET

There are many who would not consider Fyne Court a garden, in the traditional sense of the word, but this special place in the Quantock Hills is, in essence and particulars, more 'wild' than any other place in this book.

Originally, this 97-acre estate belonged to the Crosse family, who created pleasure grounds including a garden and arboretum around the large country house in the late 18th century. Andrew Crosse, who was dubbed the 'Wizard of Broomfield' and the 'Thunder and Lightning Man' conducted experiments in electricity here in the early 19th century. He merrily electrocuted unsuspecting friends, and strung out hundreds of metres of copper wire around the gardens, frightening the locals with the flashes and bangs that would emanate from the music room where he worked.

Records of his work and family manuscripts were lost when the house was destroyed by fire in 1894, thought to have started when a maid left a candle unattended. The blaze ripped through the building, leaving most of it in such a state it had to be torn down. It was never rebuilt. Instead, throughout the 20th century, the estate passed through various ownerships. In the intervening years, the garden and parkland were abandoned and left to nature.

Given to the National Trust in 1972, this lost garden has been sensitively managed with nature in mind. With a variety of habitats including broad-leaved woodland, ponds and meadows, it is a haven for wildlife, from rare invertebrates and pollinators, to great crested newts, birds such as greater spotted woodpeckers and nuthatches, and roe deer. More than 100 species of fungi have also been identified.

Appreciating this overgrown kingdom of brambles and nettles might take some adjustment for garden lovers, but the well-laid and edged paths through the woods prevent any impression of neglect, and there is plenty for open-minded explorers to enjoy on any of the three trails around the site.

As well as a folly of a crenellated castle, and a brooding boathouse by a woodland stream, there are also a few more recent feature introductions dotted throughout. A fallen tree, lightly carved with swirling lines to follow its natural shape, is ripe for climbing. Further along lies the sky glade, where slices of tree trunk are set standing in a ring, like a wooden stone circle. Engraved with the names of clouds and stars,

they are the perfect support for leaning back to contemplate the skies above.

In the old walled garden with its resilient red-brick walls, grass and wild flowers have been allowed to flourish in a community where native flowers like teasel, common knapweed and yarrow rub shoulders with quick-colonising interlopers such as butterfly bush and rosebay willowherb, which are always ready to take advantage.

A broad platform over part of the dipping pond further along is carved with images and names of what you might see in and around the water. These sorts of considered details ensure that the experience of Fyne Court is not that of an abandoned and uncared-for place, but one that, in being intentionally left mostly to its own devices, has been enabled to develop its truly wild character.

GREAT DIXTER, SUSSEX

The highly orchestrated, labour-intensive garden at Great Dixter is at the opposite end of the spectrum to Fyne Court's rewilded landscape. Such a heavily cultivated place seems an unlikely wildlife magnet. The gardeners here practise a layered system with successional planting, constantly adding and removing flowering plants as they peak or go over, to create high-impact schemes and colourful pot displays that bloom from spring all the way to winter.

This experimental planting design, with often clashing combinations, is legendary. Christopher Lloyd made the garden famous through his books, such as *The Well-Tempered Garden*, and his weekly *Country Life* magazine column, which ran for 40 years. His mixed planting schemes, he wrote, included 'shrubs, climbers, hardy and tender perennials, annuals and biennials, all growing together and contributing to the overall tapestry'. The trees and shrubs provide background structure, while the perennials offer stalwart interest through the season, augmented by bulbs early on, and pot-grown annuals which are popped in later. Self-sown biennials loosen everything up with some welcome spontaneity.

It wasn't always so vibrant. There was no garden when Nathaniel and Daisy Lloyd bought the 15th-century house with its estate and farm in 1910, so they asked architect Edwin Lutyens, who also restored and extended the manor, to design the gardens. He laid them out around the house, using the infrastructure of the buildings to create a series of garden rooms.

Christopher, the Lloyds's youngest son, came back here to live in the 1950s and dedicated himself to plants and the garden, developing spaces like the Barn, Sunk and Peacock Gardens, the Long Border, Topiary Lawn, Exotic Garden and Vegetable Garden, among others. 'Christo', as he was known, passed away in 2006, and his head gardener Fergus Garrett has since continued with their vision, setting up a trust to support the garden and inform and educate gardeners on the Dixter approach.

In the past 10 years, Fergus and his team purposefully stepped up sustainable practices. They stopped spraying with herbicides and pesticides, and composted more to reduce waste and create nutritious mulch and growing medium. They let the grass grow to different lengths, and clipped the hedges less often. They left deadwood standing, where possible, and turned pasture to meadow. Insect hotels and turf-and-sand roofs were created, and the skeletons of herbaceous perennials were left up over winter to offer seed heads for birds.

Curious, and with an instinct that the garden was harbouring an array of wildlife, Fergus had some initial surveys done to count the bumblebees, butterflies and moths in the garden and estate. The results were so impressive that he decided to get a spider one done too, but was surprised at how

Left The Peacock Garden with its eponymous topiary, alliums, Welsh poppies and cow parsley.

Opposite At Dixter, the intensively cultivated Long Border sits alongside a wilder meadow area where the grass is left to grow long.

difficult it was to get anyone to oblige. Ecologists just weren't all that interested in gardens, and seemed to consider them almost worthless as habitat. When he did persuade the British Arachnological Society to come, they were amazed to find a huge variety of spiders resident, including some quite rare species.

These few surveys weren't enough for Fergus, however. Buoyed by this success, he wanted to do a full, joined-up biodiversity audit, to find out about everything that was living at Dixter, which could then inform how the land was managed. A large multidisciplinary team was commissioned to survey all the different areas of the estate, from the woodland and meadows to the flower gardens and ponds. They found that the wider estate was wildlife rich, with huge numbers of breeding birds, including some species of high conservation concern such as nightingales, lesser spotted woodpeckers and song thrushes. There were also many types of bee, including the rare oak mining bee and the declining long-horned bee; unusual moths and butterflies such as the purple emperor; and a large population of great crested newts. The broad range of habitat areas overlapped and fed into each other, creating a wonderful mosaic habitat, which, as was expected, benefited a wide array of species.

What was surprising for the ecologists – gobsmacking, in fact – was that the intensively managed ornamental garden areas showed the greatest diversity. Completely unintentionally, without making any concerted effort to do so, Fergus and his team were providing a wonderfully nurturing and nourishing place for wildlife. Those high-maintenance, ever-changing, always-blooming borders offered a feast of nectar and pollen over a very long season, encouraging swarms of pollinators.

There were also a multitude of places for a multitude of things to live and breed, from old buildings where bats could roost to old walls where solitary bees could nest. There was deep and shallow water, which was both planted and unplanted, and scrubby areas, muddy areas and piles of deadwood. The lead ecologist, originally unconvinced of the value of the garden, now calls it a 'garden nature reserve', and says Dixter is 'a masterclass in how to bring biodiversity conservation into modern-day horticulture'.

It can give all us gardeners heart that gardens, whether large or small, can be a fantastic resource for wildlife, and an important tool in conserving, maintaining and even increasing biodiversity.

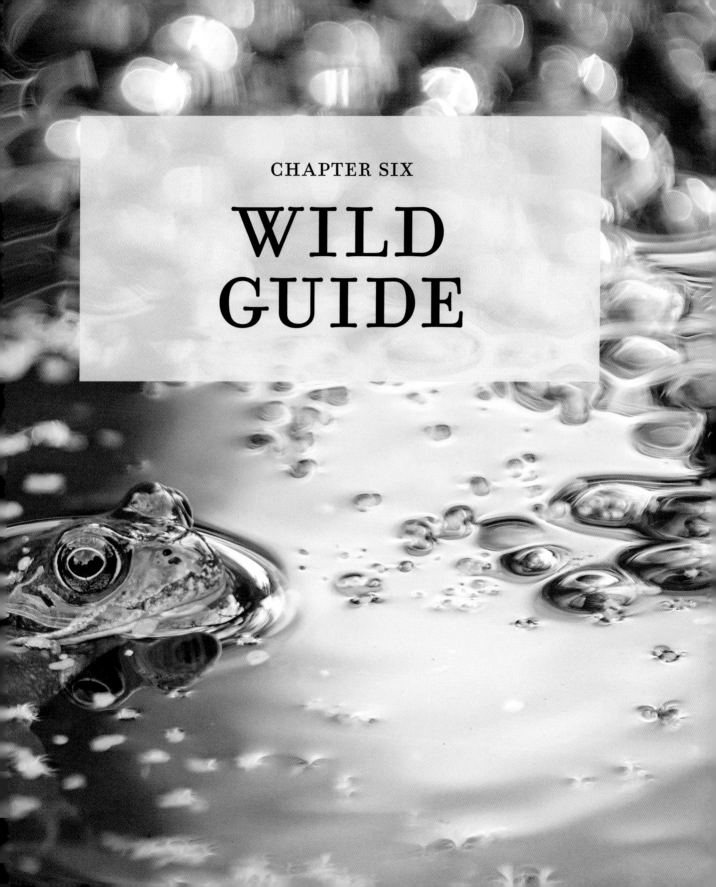

CHAPTER SIX

WILD GUIDE

Top tips and advice on ways to create and manage a wildlife-friendly garden.

Private gardens cover around 1.2 million acres in the UK – that's about one-fifth the size of Wales, and an area bigger than all of the UK's National Nature Reserves combined. In cities, half of the green space is made up of gardens. It seems obvious that harnessing the potential of this land for conservation could be a game changer, a way to turn the tide on species and habitat loss. Unfortunately, it's a bit more complicated than that.

Most gardens are small, and they are separated from each other, and other green space, by barriers like buildings, walls, fences, footpaths, streets and roads. They cannot compensate for the large tracts of countryside that have been and are being lost, which support wild native plants and insects, and larger birds and mammals. They can't replace specific habitats like oak woodland or chalk grassland and their unique networks of adapted organisms.

They can, however, help to maintain biodiversity and operate as another type of habitat, where some things live, but others simply visit to feed or use as a rest stop on the way to somewhere else. If you decide to garden in a way that does no harm, and offer food and shelter, your garden can still be a really valuable resource for wildlife.

This is not intended to be an exhaustive guide on how to attract wildlife in your garden. Instead, these are key tips and pointers to get you started. If you understand these core principles, you can use them as the basis from which to make decisions about your garden, armed with the background philosophy and basics of wild gardening.

This might hurt a little

Gardening for wildlife means learning how to share. If you want wild things to make themselves at home in your garden, then you have to make space for them – and that includes head space as well as physical space. The transition from neat and tidy gardener, in control of all you survey, to wildlife-enabling cohabitee can be challenging. Whether you want to call it 'ungardening' or 'rewilding', gardening for wildlife means resisting the urge to tidy up, and growing plants you may not find as attractive, well-behaved or useful, and accepting imperfections like holey leaves. It means choosing ethics over aesthetics. But the reward for embracing this alternative vision of beauty is an endlessly fascinating garden brimming with life.

Top left Blackbirds prefer to eat off the ground or a feeding table.

Top right As well as a drinking source, garden birds like a shallow water feature so they can bathe and preen their feathers.

Bottom left Attract goldfinches with a feeder full of nyger seed.

Bottom right Put up nest boxes for birds like blue tits in your garden.

Start small, but think big

A wildlife garden is a community of species with often interdependent relationships. Use this to your advantage. Garden in a way that creates a healthy soil, which will sustain the plants you introduce, which will attract insects, which will then attract birds and small animals, which may in turn attract bigger animals. If you first provide for the little guys, they will form the building blocks of a living structure, a network of connections from the smallest microbe to the large bird of prey, creating an ecosystem that benefits them all.

The flip side of this is that a change or action affecting one part of the network can have an impact on the other parts, so you must be careful when and how you intervene, and not assume you can pick and choose which wildlife you want to visit. You might like bees and butterflies, not spiders or caterpillars, but making a garden for wildlife means accepting the part every thing has to play in the wider ecosystem. That moss you'd like to get rid of is an essential material for wrens building their nests. Some of those caterpillars that are eating through your prized plants will become food for hungry baby blue tits and hedgehogs, and the ones that escape will become butterflies and moths that pollinate your plants, and become food for birds and bats.

Try to understand the entire life cycles of the plants and creatures in your garden, and learn how they all interact with each other, before taking action on something you see as undesirable.

Softly, softly

The design of a garden doesn't matter much to your wildlife visitors, but what does have an impact is the amount of hard versus soft landscaping. The more hard surfaces there are in a garden, such as paving and fences, the less wildlife there is. Consider reducing the size of your patio and pathways, or, if starting from scratch, minimise them as much as possible.

For patios and paths, think about using gravel instead of poured concrete or pavers, or leave the gaps between pavers free of jointing compound or cement grout – miner and mason bees particularly love these cracks and crannies. These joints could also be planted with flowering creeping thyme, chamomile or mind-your-own-business to maximise every bit of space with planting.

In the same vein, the nooks and crevices of dry-stone walls or stone-filled gabion baskets are wonderful hangouts for garden invertebrates like insects and spiders, small mammals like voles and shrews, reptiles like slow-worms, and amphibians like frogs and newts.

Opposite left Robins may nest on or near the ground so keep a look out in hedges, nooks and hollows.

Opposite right Create your own bug hotels with scrap wood like these homes for solitary bees.

Above left Wild gardeners would be delighted to find a slow-worm in their plots.

Above right Blackthorn blossom is a good spring nectar source for butterflies.

Instead of pointed solid walls or fences, make boundaries from hedges, preferably mixed native hedging or hawthorn – the ultimate wildlife plant, which provides food for more than 150 different insect species. If the walls or fences are already in place, growing climbers like honeysuckle, early clematis, jasmine and roses up and over them is an excellent way to add a layer of flower and fruit and green up vertical spaces. In small gardens where hedges and large shrubs are not possible, climbers can provide the same attributes but in a fraction of the footprint.

If you plant it, they will come

The more plants, and the more diverse the variety of plants in a garden, the more wildlife there will be. Gardens with large woody plants – that is, trees and shrubs – have been shown to encourage the most biodiversity. If you don't have one already, plant a tree, or two if there is room (do check the eventual height and spread before buying). An apple tree is a good choice, with a multitude of benefits, from blossom and fruit to a place for birds to nest and perch, and is suitable even for small gardens. Maybe

you won't see your tree grow all the way to maturity, but it is a wonderful investment in the future. To paraphrase an old adage, the best time to plant a tree was 20 years ago, but the second-best time is today.

The next layer can be shrubs like *Ribes odoratum*, elder and spindleberry for berries, and hazel for nuts, as well as climbers like common honeysuckle and climbing or rambling roses, which create shelter, have nectar-rich flowers in summer and berries or hips in autumn.

When choosing plants for pollinators, think about those that flower over as long a season as possible, because the more flowers there are in a garden, the higher the number of pollinating insects. Consider winter-flowering shrubs like Japanese quince, heather, witch hazel and sweet box, as well as those with catkins, like pussy willow and hazel. We usually consider ivy to be a climber, but when it matures past its juvenile phase (which can take quite a few years), it looks more like an evergreen shrub, and starts to produce flowers and berries that are a fantastic early food source for insects and birds.

In autumn, plant as many spring-flowering bulbs as you can. Blooms like snowdrops, daffodils and

crocuses are immensely important for pollinators that emerge early, like queen bumblebees and mining bees, red mason bees, hairy-footed flower bees and many hoverflies and butterflies. Make sure to have some native and near-native spring flowers too, like primroses, sweet violets, lungworts, forget-me-nots, foxgloves and viper's bugloss, to create a nectar banquet for a broad range of British insects.

Top summer perennials that are proven to attract pollinators include catmint 'Six Hills Giant', *Geranium* 'Rozanne' and lavender 'Gros Bleu', and to extend the season, late-summer-flowering *Dahlia* 'Bishop of Llandaff' and *Helenium* 'Moerheim Beauty', which keep going into autumn. You can sow annuals such as cosmos and sunflowers, and herbs including wild marjoram, comfrey 'Bocking 14' and borage are also great. In general,

aim to use single, simple flowers that are easy for pollinators to access, rather than intricate double (usually sterile) forms.

Butterflies will make a beeline for buddleia, scabious, verbena, sedums and asters. Moths love mint, rosebay willowherb, valerian and night-active plants such as night-scented stock. Although these flowers are packed with nectar, they don't provide the forage needed to support breeding, so to encourage our fluttering friends to lay eggs, and to provide food for those hungry, hungry caterpillars and moth larvae, use plants such as mullein, *Cirsium* thistle, fuchsia and hops. They will get chomped and may end up with leaves like lace doilies, but that's the price to pay, and it's worth it.

If you have a big garden, consider leaving a patch of nettles to grow, to support peacock, red admiral,

tortoiseshell and many other butterflies – but with the caveat that it has to be a large block, and in the sun, to be in any way beneficial. Brambles are another excellent wild plant better suited to large wildlife gardens, where they can create the perfect margins with meadow or woodland areas.

Instead of cutting your borders and beds back to the ground in autumn, leave some herbaceous perennials standing over winter, for cover, and seed heads to feed birds and small mammals. They give

great visual structure to the garden throughout the cold months and look beautiful rimed with frost, as well as keeping down weeds and protecting all the microbes, insects and earthworms that live in the soil. You can cut down the dead stalks in early spring, just as new growth starts to show at the base, so the soil is covered for as much of the year as possible. Plants with good winter form and the best seed heads include species of *Rudbeckia*, coneflower, yarrow, bear's breeches, globe thistle and *Liatris*.

Opposite left Flowering spring bulbs such as crocuses are an excellent nectar source for early flying bees.

Opposite right Grow lots of pollinator plants like catmint to attract butterflies such as this painted lady.

Above left Grow forage plants and allow caterpillars like this mullein moth to munch at will.

Above right Leaving flowers to go to seed in the garden provides birds with an important food source.

Just add water

If you do just one thing to make your garden wildlife-friendly, introduce water. Ponds are an amazing habitat for insects and aquatic creatures like toads, but they are also a drinking source and food buffet for plenty of other garden animals. They should be designed so there are shallow edges, sloping down to a depth of about 45cm in the centre. Add aquatic and marginal plants such as water lilies and loosestrife that love wet and damp conditions, and make sure to clear the pond out every few years. If you don't have room for a pond, a small container with some aquatic plants will work too – just ensure it has at least one sloping side for access. Even a shallow bird bath can offer welcome respite for all manner of creatures.

Above left Frogs will flock to water features and ponds – ensure the sides are sloped so they can get in and out.

Above right Bats and other creatures use water features for drinking and feeding too.

Opposite Cut a path through long grass so both you and wildlife can get the most out of it.

Let it go

Another easy way to make a big difference in your garden is to leave the mower in the shed and let your grass grow long. Our lawns can be home to around 200 species of flowers – most commonly dandelion, daisy, selfheal and white clover – and, if left to flower, they could produce enough nectar to support the equivalent of 400 bees a day. The best results are with the 'Mohican' cut, with two different heights of grass. The shorter sward, cut once a month to a height of about 4–5cm, will have the most flowers, and therefore nectar; while longer grass left uncut all season has a broader range of species.

Mowing a neat path through or around the area helps to signal that this is an intentional choice rather than laziness, but if your neighbours are looking at it askance, put up a notice such as a Blue Campaign heart sign, and see if you can share with them the benefits of gardening for wildlife. When it comes to cutting back the long grass at the end of the season, beat it gently before strimming to scare off creatures like slow-worms and frogs.

Another element you can leave to grow a bit shaggier are hedges. Many will produce nutritious flowers and fruit if left unpruned, but even those that don't should be clipped as infrequently as possible – some gardeners clip every other year or one side only every year – and only once birds have flown the nest in summer. It's the same for shrubs: let them find their own natural form and intervene as rarely as you can.

Top left Hedgehogs love undisturbed cavities and leaf piles in the garden.

Top right Attract ladybirds to your garden with pollen-rich plants and they will help keep down pests like greenfly.

Bottom Save money and the planet by composting garden waste and making your own 'black gold'.

Pile it high

Garden dwellers love a good pile. Moths flock to open compost heaps; solitary bees like a nice mound of soil; and hedgehogs adore a stack of logs. A really good wildlife pile will have stacked softwood and hardwood logs, big and small, with bark on. Place them in the shade, with some in contact with or part buried in the ground, and you can add leaf piles or branches if you like. As well as a shelter for hibernating hedgehogs and other small mammals and amphibians, these piles of lying deadwood are essential habitats for boring insects and invertebrates including many beetles, and fungi, which play a vital role in breaking down this material into soil and nutrients.

Put aside the 'cides

It's obvious that gardening with wildlife in mind means gardening without chemicals like pesticides and herbicides, which means finding other ways to deal with pests, diseases and weeds. Often it's about accepting that these things will happen and trying to find smart solutions to achieve a natural balance. For example, if aphids are all over your roses, plant more things to attract ladybirds, so they can gobble some up for you.

An extra word of caution when it comes to chemicals – organic gardening and wildlife gardening are obvious partners, but they are not the same thing. Many organic pesticides, and products like organic slug pellets, might still be harmful to wild things. Check carefully or simply avoid using them altogether, and think more broadly about all chemicals you bring into the garden, from plant feed to paint. What is really necessary? What can you make yourself within the garden, or do without?

Sustainable steps

Wildlife gardening goes hand in hand with sustainable gardening. It makes sense that as well as encouraging wildlife in the garden, we make efforts to reduce the resources we use and the impact on wildlife out in the wider world.

Firstly, plant to suit your conditions, so you don't need to do additional feeding and watering, and try to disturb the soil as little as possible. One big thing you can do is not buy growing mediums containing peat. The continuing extraction of peat is destroying irreplaceable peat bog habitats that lots of wildlife depend on, and it releases tonnes of carbon dioxide

into the atmosphere. There are many peat-free alternatives available for container plants, and to top up beds you can use compost created from your garden waste. Also, when you buy plants, source them from suppliers and nurseries that grow peat-free and without pesticides.

Consider all the landscaping materials you use – how long will they last, and when they break down will they contaminate the soil? Are the surfaces permeable, so that water can percolate down into the ground, or will it instead run off the top into storm drains and contribute to flooding and pollution?

Find alternatives to non-recyclable black plastic pots, support nurseries that do too, and reuse the ones you have already, so that more plastic waste doesn't end up polluting our soil and oceans and killing wildlife.

Keep your garden waste within the garden by reusing, repairing and recycling materials, tools and utensils, and creating compost and leaf mould to spread as nutritious mulch. For larger gardens, a garden shredder is invaluable for breaking down tougher stems and small branches quickly.

With climate change, wet winters and dry summers are set to become the norm in many areas, so add water butts to your downpipes to capture rainwater to use instead of mains water.

This cyclical approach is the best way to make your garden low-impact, sustainable and resilient – think of it as future-proofing.

Beyond your backyard

It's wonderful to have your own little patch of paradise, but a garden is most valuable for wildlife when it's part of a larger area of green space. Your garden and your neighbours' gardens, the street trees, nearby road verges, parks and brownfield sites, can be linked up to create more beneficial wildlife corridors.

Find out how your local authority is managing your local green spaces. Are they letting the grass grow long where they can, or still using hothouse bedding plants each summer? Are they spraying herbicides on footpaths and kerbs or letting pavement plants flower? Are they planning to build a new estate development or shopping centre on a piece of land that is a species-rich habitat?

Perhaps with the right influence and support, your area could become a leader in wildlife conservation. But to make a big difference, we all need to get involved with the bigger issues beyond our backyards, advocate for wildlife and make sure local and national government know how important these issues are to us, and for the future of all living things.

WILD GARDENS TO VISIT

Barn Garden
The Barn, Serge Hill Lane, Abbots Langley,
Hertfordshire, WD5 0RZ
info@tomstuartsmith.co.uk

Beth Chatto Gardens
Elmstead Market, Colchester, Essex, CO7 7DB
info@bethchatto.co.uk

Bodnant Garden
Tal-y-Cafn, near Colwyn Bay, Conwy, LL28 5RE
bodnantgarden@nationaltrust.org.uk

Colby Woodland Garden
Near Amroth, Pembrokeshire, SA67 8PP
colby@nationaltrust.org.uk

Coleton Fishacre
Brownstone Road, Kingswear, Devon, TQ6 0EQ
coletonfishacre@nationaltrust.org.uk

Fyne Court
Broomfield, Bridgwater, Somerset, TA5 2EQ
fynecourt@nationaltrust.org.uk

Glendurgan Garden
Mawnan Smith, near Falmouth, Cornwall, TR11 5JZ
glendurgan@nationaltrust.org.uk

Gravetye Manor
Vowels Lane, West Hoathly, Sussex, RH19 4LJ
info@gravetyemanor.co.uk

Great Chalfield Manor and Garden
Near Melksham, Wiltshire, SN12 8NH
greatchalfieldmanor@nationaltrust.org.uk

Great Dixter House & Gardens
Northiam, Rye, East Sussex, TN31 6PH
office@greatdixter.co.uk

Hill Top
Near Sawrey, Hawkshead, Ambleside, Cumbria,
LA22 0LF
hilltop@nationaltrust.org.uk

Lowther Castle
Penrith, Cumbria, CA10 2HH
info@lowthercastle.org

Prospect Cottage
Dungeness Rd, Dungeness, Romney Marsh,
Kent, TN29 9NE

Scotney Castle
Lamberhurst, Tunbridge Wells, Kent, TN3 8JB
scotneycastle@nationaltrust.org.uk

Sheringham Park

Upper Sheringham, Norfolk, NR26 8TL

sheringhampark@nationaltrust.org.uk

Sissinghurst Castle Garden

Biddenden Road, near Cranbrook, Kent, TN17 2AB

sissinghurst@nationaltrust.org.uk

Stowe

Buckingham, Buckinghamshire, MK18 5EQ

stowe@nationaltrust.org.uk

Trengwainton Garden

Madron, near Penzance, Cornwall, TR20 8RZ

trengwainton@nationaltrust.org.uk

Waltham Place

Church Hill, White Waltham, Berkshire, SL6 3JH

estateoffice@walthamplace.com

The Weir Garden

Swainshill, Hereford, Herefordshire, HR4 7QF

theweir@nationaltrust.org.uk

Wildside

Green Lane, Buckland Monachorum, Devon, PL20 7NP

wileyatwildside.com

USEFUL RESOURCES

Bat Conservation Trust
www.bats.org.uk

British Hedgehog Preservation Society
www.britishhedgehogs.org.uk

Buglife – The Invertebrate Conservation Trust
www.buglife.org.uk

Bumblebee Conservation Trust
www.bumblebeeconservation.org

Butterfly Conservation
www.butterfly-conservation.org

Grow Wild
www.growwilduk.com

National Trust
www.nationaltrust.org.uk

The Orchard Project
www.theorchardproject.org.uk

People's Trust for Endangered Species
www.ptes.org

Plantlife – The Wild Plant Conservation Charity
www.plantlife.org.uk

Royal Society for the Protection of Birds
www.rspb.org.uk

The Wildlife Trusts
www.wildlifetrusts.org

The Woodland Trust
www.woodlandtrust.org.uk

INDEX

Right Roses clamber up the trees in the orchard meadow at Sissinghurst Castle Garden in Kent.

PICTURE CREDITS

Opposite Drought-tolerant planting in the Gravel Garden at the Beth Chatto Gardens in Essex.

ACKNOWLEDGEMENTS

I'm grateful to Peter Taylor and Claire Masset for commissioning me and David Salmo for his excellent editing. Thank you to all the people who gave up their time to be interviewed, give garden tours and answer questions, in particular Tom Stuart-Smith, Dan Pearson, Asa Gregers-Warg, Tom Coward, Pete Tasker, Patsy Floyd, Keith Wiley, Fergus Garrett, Mikko Moran, John Rippin, Mark Webster, Andre Tranquilini and Niki McCann.

Special thanks to my wonderful parents and siblings for their constant support and cheerleading (so loud it can sometimes be heard across the Irish Sea).

This book is dedicated to John – maker of tea, giver of pep talks, bringer of wine – and in memory of dearest, sweetest Paddy, who was there for all our adventures.

Below The maze at Glendurgan Garden in Cornwall below a bank of bluebells and wild garlic.